Acting Lessons
for Teachers

Acting Lessons for Teachers

Using Performance Skills in the Classroom

Robert T. Tauber and
Cathy Sargent Mester

PRAEGER

Westport, Connecticut
London

Library of Congress Cataloging-in-Publication Data

Tauber, Robert T.
    Acting lessons for teachers : using performance skills in the
classroom / Robert T. Tauber and Cathy Sargent Mester.
        p. cm.
    Includes bibliographical references and index.
    ISBN 0–275–94823–4 (alk. paper).—ISBN 0–275–94824–2 (pbk. :
alk. paper)
    1. Teachers—Training of.   2. Acting—Study and teaching.
3. Communication in education.   I. Mester, Cathy Sargent.
II. Title.
LB1732.T38   1994
370.71—dc20   94–13736

British Library Cataloguing in Publication Data is available.

Library of Congress Catalog Card Number: 94–13736
ISBN: 0–275–94823–4
        0–275–94824–2 (pbk.)

First published in 1994

Praeger Publishers, 88 Post Road West, Westport, CT 06881
An imprint of Greenwood Publishing Group, Inc.

Printed in the United States of America

∞™

The paper used in this book complies with the
Permanent Paper Standard issued by the National
Information Standards Organization (Z39.48–1984).

10 9 8 7 6 5 4 3 2

CONTENTS

Contents   xi

ILLUSTRATIONS

Acknowledgments

We want to thank both the theorists and practitioners who, through their earlier work in the form of conference papers and published articles, provided much of the research and practice upon which this book is based. We also want to thank Stephen C. Buckwald who, early in the development of this project, helped brainstorm acting/teaching ideas. Finally, we owe a debt of gratitude to the award-winning college professors who contributed original selections for this book.

Special thanks are offered to Wendy Gouldthorpe Eidenmuller, one of our Division secretaries, who willingly read and marked drafts, as well as typeset, this book. Without her dedication, this book would not have been possible. Finally, we want to thank our families for their unwavering support.

R.T.T.
C.S.M.

PART I

BACKGROUND

CHAPTER 1

TEACHER ENTHUSIASM: A PEDAGOGICAL NECESSITY

> Nothing great was ever accomplished without enthusiasm!
> —Emerson

TEACHER ENTHUSIASM: ITS RELATIONSHIP TO PEDAGOGY

It is Wednesday morning, 9:00 AM. Faculty and staff have gathered for an inservice program. Some teachers have a cup of coffee; others have coffee and doughnuts. The stage is set for a morning of "inservicing"! The workshop leader welcomes the educators, then asks them to read a series of quotations handwritten on poster board in large print that he tapes, one at a time, to the walls of the classroom. Two sides of the room are needed to display the eight or nine quotations. Participants then are asked to determine the message that is common in each of the displayed quotations. The task is not difficult.

Among the quotations hung on the wall are:

- *Enthusiasm* is the key to being a successful teacher (Soenksen 1992).
- Effective teachers motivate their students with an *enthusiastic* style of teaching (Brophy and Good 1986).
- One of the five delivery characteristics associated with effective teaching is the projection of *enthusiasm* for the subject matter (Goulden 1991).
- A great teacher qua teacher—as opposed to scholar or ethical exemplar or authority figure—has intensity and communicates it *enthusiastically* (Hanning 1984).
- The outstanding feature of effective teaching is the ability to communicate effectively. Put another way, a good teacher is a good talker—one who exemplifies *enthusiasm* for his or her work (Schwartz 1980).
- One of twelve affinity-seeking strategies used by teachers that is associated with competence and motivation is dynamism—physically indicating to students that one is dynamic, active, and *enthusiastic* (Frymier and Thompson 1992).

- What constitutes masterful teaching? A factor found prominent in most studies is the instructor's ability to stimulate *enthusiasm* for the subject, a skill frequently related to the teacher's personal *enthusiasm* (Lowman 1984).
- A teacher who is not able to convey *enthusiasm* for his or her subject (even though he may feel it inwardly) labors under a great handicap. Students are unwilling to accept a teacher who cannot transmit to them something of the excitement of his or her field (Jordan 1982).

A great teacher is not just someone who is approachable as a person, although this is not an uncommon characteristic of a great teacher. A great teacher also isn't simply a scholar—one who knows a lot—although knowing a lot about one's field certainly can contribute to greatness. What one knows must be communicated. Jordan (1982, 124) reminds us that "the Teacher as Scholar is important, that the Teacher as Person is crucial, and that the Teacher as Communicator is indispensable." Teacher enthusiasm, the common factor in the displayed quotations, is fundamental to effective communication.

The workshop leader continues by stating that teacher enthusiasm is a pedagogical necessity. Cautious, but slightly nervous, participants agree. One participant, though, volunteers that classrooms do not just contain teachers; they contain students, too. Therefore, one might argue—in fact, one should argue—that enthusiastic teaching is of little value unless effective student learning takes place. Measures of effective learning consist of heightened student interest, positive student attitude, more on-task student behavior, and greater student achievement, among other factors.

We would argue that effective actors, too, must communicate what they know. But, unlike teachers, actors have long recognized the need to develop specific skills, especially means and methods of expression, to enhance their communication. The bulk of this book is devoted to helping teachers develop acting skills that can help them communicate better.

TEACHER ENTHUSIASM: ITS RELATIONSHIP TO STUDENT ACHIEVEMENT

At this point, the workshop leader asks those gathered to read the remaining quotations, prepared as handwritten signs that he also tapes, one at a time, on the remaining two walls of the classroom. Among the quotations displayed are:

- Teachers' enthusiasm has been found to be related [positively] to student achievement gains (Rosenshine and Furst 1973).
- Children taught at a high level of enthusiasm were more attentive, interested, and responsive (Burts et al. 1985).

- Student rating scores were significantly higher for expressive than for nonexpressive [enthusiastic] lectures (Meier and Feldhusen 1979).

- Research has shown correlational and causal links between teacher enthusiasm and student achievement (Gillett 1980).

- Teachers who received enthusiasm training had students who demonstrated a more positive attitude toward reading (Streeter 1986).

- Teachers trained in how to enhance their enthusiasm had students whose on-task time was significantly greater than for non-trained teachers (Bettencourt, Gillett, and Hull 1983).

- Teachers receiving training in how to be more enthusiastic had LD students who scored substantially higher on post-tests and exhibited more acceptable classroom behaviors (Brigham 1991).

- Students repeatedly indicate that they learn more from those who evince enthusiasm and concern for the quality of teaching, even though they may frequently complain about their own required extra effort (Browne and Keeley 1985).

The connection between teacher enthusiasm and desired student learning outcomes is clear. Researchers document it; practitioners testify to it. Teacher enthusiasm is one means to the end of greater student achievement.

Another point that emerges from these quotations is that teacher enthusiasm is a quality associated with effective teaching across all disciplines, all grade levels, and all categories of students. Teacher enthusiasm is as important in English as it is in physics, as important in social studies as it is in mathematics. "Regardless of content, the college classroom does not have to be agonizingly dull" (Welsz 1990, 74). The same point applies to all classrooms.

Figure 1.1 depicts the central role that enthusiasm plays in holding students' attention, generating students' interest, and developing students' positive attitudes toward learning. Highly enthusiastic teachers are highly expressive in vocal delivery, gestures, body movement, and overall energy level. All of these are crucial ingredients that, in turn, contribute to greater student achievement.

In addition to producing greater student achievement, highly expressive (enthusiastic) teachers tend to have students who attribute their higher student achievement to "their own attributes—namely, ability and effort" (Perry 1985, 44). Given that the attributions of "ability" and "effort" are internal—within students' own power to influence—one would expect students who develop such attributions to experience still greater achievement in the future. After all, these students perceive the world, now, as more controllable. A circle, then, of greater student achievement credited to ability and effort leading to more student achievement has been created—all influenced by enthusiastic teachers.

Figure 1.1
Teacher Enthusiasm and Student Achievement

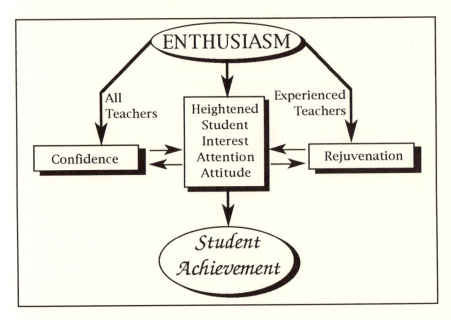

Eison (1990) believes that in the classroom, a teacher's enthusiasm is often contagious; so too is his or her lack of enthusiasm. He believes that "enthusiasm and energy can carry the day" (p. 24). Who has not personally experienced the infectious enthusiasm generated by singers in an outdoor concert (e.g., the Beach Boys), by a well-performed Nutcracker Suite, or by a stirring symphony and its conductor? That same infectious enthusiasm can exist in classrooms.

McKeachie, a recognized name in the field of pedagogy, claims that probably no one characteristic is more important in education than a teacher's enthusiasm and energy (1986). Lowman (1984) argues that a factor found prominently in most research on teaching effectiveness is the instructor's ability to stimulate enthusiasm for the subject—a skill often related to the teacher's perceived enthusiasm. Sincere enthusiasm helps create, as well as maintain, a good learning environment (Campbell 1981). Teacher enthusiasm has a positive impact—greater student achievement—on kindergarten youngsters, college students, and all those in between. The evidence is overwhelming in favor of teacher enthusiasm!

SUMMARY

A teacher's zest for teaching, like an actor's zeal for acting, is revealed in his or her displayed enthusiasm. It is obvious in his or her expressiveness. Weimer (1993), in her book *Improving Your Classroom Teaching*, devotes an entire chapter to the importance of enthusiasm. Early in the chapter she boldly declares, "Enthusiasm: Do It!" She states that one should not try to be enthusiastic. One should, instead, focus upon things that will convey your enthusiasm to the class. We agree.

In thinking about the parallel between acting and teaching, and the common denominator, enthusiasm, other "e" words come to mind. Among them are expressing, exhilarating, exciting, enlightening, enthralling, and, for that matter, even entertaining. A stage production or movie described this way would signal a dramatic or cinematic success. It would be a credit to the actors. A classroom characterized this way, similarly, would be a "hit" and a credit to the teacher. Exactly how teachers or professors are supposed to convey their enthusiasm is the emphasis of the book you are reading.

CHAPTER 2

BOOSTING TEACHER ENTHUSIASM: A CRAFTSPERSON'S TOOLBOX

It is not *who* you are but *what* you do that conveys enthusiasm.
— Anonymous

BOOSTING TEACHER EFFECTIVENESS THROUGH PERFORMING

The point of chapter 1 was that more effective teachers are perceived as more enthusiastic teachers. Teacher enthusiasm, in turn, often leads to greater student achievement. The question, now, is how can teachers become more enthusiastic? As the quotation at the beginning of this chapter says, "It is not *who* you are but *what* you do that conveys enthusiasm."

Years ago, one of the authors supervised student teachers. Prior to entering the classroom for the first time, many of these student teachers had bouts of severe anxiety — they had the actor's version of stage fright. In an effort to calm their nerves, the author reassuringly offered this profound statement: "Don't worry. Just go in there, and be yourself." In hindsight, this was terrible advice to give because many of these student teachers were, in fact, rather boring people. If they went into the classroom and "remained themselves," they would have been boring teachers. We can't imagine a director telling stage-frightened actors to just go on stage and "be themselves."

According to Hanning (1984, 33), "You [teachers] don't have a 'self' to be when you start out as a teacher; that is you don't have a teacher-self. You have to develop one, and you do that by acting a part, by performing a role . . . as you would (in) a theatre." Teachers should present their subject matter in much the same way effective salespersons and performing artists do. Teachers can enhance their versatility by using the same tools of the trade as performing artists.

At first glance performing a role — acting a part — may appear out of place to some educators. It shouldn't. In many ways, teaching in the classroom is not unlike acting on the stage or in the cinema. In both the theater and the classroom, the character on stage must hold the attention of the listeners by using a variety of captivating devices. Teachers have the additional burden of having to hold the attention of their audiences 180 days a year!

According to Lowman (1984, 11), "classrooms are fundamentally arenas in which the teacher is the focal point, just as the actor or orator is on a stage — teaching is undeniably a performing art." He further argues that, like other performers, teachers must convey a strong stage presence, often using overt enthusiasm, animation, and humor to accomplish this goal. Rubin (1985, 100), too, argues that "teaching was (is) a performing art" and supports this belief by including chapters titled "The Classroom as Theatre," "Teacher as Actor," and "Lesson Staging."

Rubin (1985) states that school, like drama, is meant to be experienced directly. When a student who has missed a class asks, "What did we do in class yesterday?" his or her teacher often is at a loss to offer an appropriate response. Although the teacher might like to say, "Gee, you really lucked out. We didn't do a thing in that class"; more often he or she responds by saying something to the effect that, "You had to be there in order to understand what happened in yesterday's class." A missed session might be described, but the real spirit of the event is missed.

Teachers act the role of teachers — a role that can, and does, vary from school to school and classroom to classroom. The classroom teacher is on stage. "The acting or performing dimension of the teaching act is highly relevant to a large portion of the teacher's role. Verve, color, humor, creativity, surprise, and even 'hamming' have characterized most great teachers" (Baughman 1979, 27).

Despite the parallel between the two professions, very little has been written about how teachers might employ techniques used by actors to develop Hanning's concept of teacher-self. Nor has much been written about theatrical or acting devices for holding the audience's attention that might be suited to that same goal in the classroom. This book attempts to address this void.

This chapter outlines a number of specific things teachers can do — most with a foundation in drama — in order to appear more enthusiastic. If educators "act" enthusiastic as teachers, over a period of time they may, in fact, "become" more enthusiastic as people.

One need only look at the world of drama in order to see people regularly acting as something they most often are not in real life. Actors constantly are developing their acting-selves in a manner similar to Hanning's recommendation that teachers develop their teacher-selves. Actors use acting skills. More successful actors more successfully use these performance skills. Teachers, too, can — and should — use these same skills. These performance skills have the potential for boosting a teacher's perceived enthusiasm.

A CRAFTSPERSON'S TOOLBOX

We envision a teacher's performance skills, his or her teaching strategies, as analogous to the tools carried by any craftsperson, including actors. This analogy is supported by Rubin (1985, 15) when he explains that the artistry part of teaching consists of "master craftsmanship." In the craftsperson's toolbox there are two categories of tools. Some tools are used more frequently and so are kept ever handy in the top tray. Other tools, used less frequently, are stored in the bottom of the craftsperson's toolbox, as in figure 2.1.

Such a variety of tools enables the knowledgeable craftsperson to have the right tool handy to accomplish the desired task. Without the right tools, always kept sharp, and the knowledge of how to use them, a craftsperson would be limited in his or her effectiveness. The same holds true for teachers.

THE CRAFTSPERSON HIMSELF OR HERSELF

Subject Matter Mastery

Although having the right tool for the job helps, a prerequisite to this is possessing the knowledge to use that tool in the first place. Tools do not operate themselves. But, even prior to knowing *how* to use a tool, one needs to know *what* tool from those available should be used in a given situation. It reminds us of students trying to solve problems in a physics course. The mathematics used in physics normally is not the stumbling block. The real difficulty for students is deciding (knowing) what formula, of the many available, best applies to the circumstances of the present problem.

The common ingredient in the above scenarios is knowledge. Actors must know their lines before they can expect to deliver them effectively. Teachers must know their subject matter before they can expect to teach it effectively to others. Subject Matter Mastery is the first acting/teaching skill that we will address. In our craftsperson analogy, Subject Matter Mastery is not something viewed as a tool to be carried in the toolbox. Subject Matter Mastery is carried in the craftsperson's head — always ready, constantly used.

Without the proper mastery of content knowledge, the delivery, no matter how exciting, becomes as Shakespeare wrote, "full of sound and fury, signifying nothing" (*Macbeth*, Act V, Scene 5). More recently, Spencer Tracy is reported to have offered this advice to an aspiring actor: "know your lines and don't bump into the furniture." Teachers must know their material.

Figure 2.1
Craftsperson's Toolbox

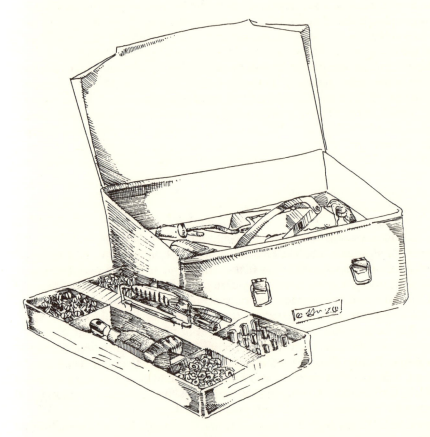

Drawing courtesy of Mark Fisher.

In an often-cited experiment, an actor, introduced to a conference audience as Dr. Fox ("The Dr. Fox Effect"), presented an enthusiastic lecture that not only contained little content but used double-talk, irrelevant and contradictory examples (Perry 1985). The audience highly rated the lecture, citing that, among other things, it stimulated their thinking. Is it possible, then, to secure and hold the attention of an audience but, in the end, deliver little in the way of content? Teachers who lack subject expertise *may* be able to use acting skills, in the famous words of Abraham Lincoln, "to fool some of the people all the time and all the people some of the time"; but those who lack subject matter knowledge will not be able to fool all the people all of the time.

The evidence is clear: enthusiastic teachers, those who are expressive in their manner and method, more regularly do earn higher student evaluations. But, as some might ask, at what expense to student learning? None! Research confirms that these same expressive teachers generally have students who exhibit higher achievement (Abrami, Leventhal, and Perry 1982). Where you find enthusiastic teachers, you find greater student achievement. These teachers are delivering the goods — the requisite content!

Educational Resources Information Center

An overlooked source for enhancing Subject Matter Mastery is ERIC, an acronym for Educational Resources Information Center. ERIC is a thirty-year-old, federally sponsored system for collecting, evaluating, abstracting, and disseminating information in education. No better system in the world exists for unlocking information in education — on any topic, in any subject area, for any grade level, and for any category of student. If it is important and it has been written about, it is in ERIC. ERIC consists of sixteen separate clearinghouses, each responsible for certain areas of subject matter, for example, Reading and Communication Skills, Handicapped and Gifted Children, Science, Mathematics, and Environmental Education, Elementary and Early Childhood. A complete list of ERIC Clearinghouses is included in Appendix I: *Sixteen ERIC Clearinghouses*.

Access to ERIC's wealth of materials is made through one of two indexes, *Resources in Education (RIE)* and *Current Index to Journals in Education (CIJE)*. The former unlocks endless "documents," for example, curriculum guides, conference proceedings, project reports; the latter unlocks articles published in more than seven-hundred, most often practitioner-friendly, education journals. With the increasing availability in nearby public and college libraries of ERIC on CD-ROM, educators can use a computer terminal to search data bases to locate subject-matter and pedagogy-related information. Educators are also encouraged to contact directly those clearinghouses that represent their disciplines.

THE CRAFTSPERSON'S TOP-TRAY TOOLS

Through both research and interviews with award-winning faculty, we have identified three acting/teaching skills that should be used regularly by teachers. They are:

- Animation: voice
- Animation: body
- Classroom space

The justification for including these three skills as top-tray tools (skills) is presented in separate chapters that follow. For now, suffice it to say that it would be unheard of for actors to ignore the importance of vocal animation (e.g., pitch, volume, voice quality, rate) in their attempts to hold an audience's attention and to get their message across. Should teachers be any less concerned about their effective use of voice? Actors take lessons and practice-practice-practice these skills. Should teachers, too, work at improving the impact of such a resource?

In like manner, no successful actor could, or would, overlook the importance of physical animation and effective use of space. The power of body language, perhaps even more convincing than verbal language, is not lost on the successful actor. Nor is the value of one's physical placement within the stage setting. Teachers, too, should be sensitive to their physical animation and use of space.

THE CRAFTSPERSON'S OTHER TOOLS

Also, through research and interviews with award-winning faculty, we have identified four acting/teaching skills that are most effective when used occasionally — whether in the theater or in the classroom. These skills include:

- Humor
- Role-playing
- Use of props
- Suspense and surprise

Once again, successful actors work long and hard at perfecting each of these skills. With respect to role playing, no doubt some actors feel more comfortable in some roles than in others. Yet, through a combination of sweat and talent, most are able to carry out many roles in a convincing manner. We believe that teachers, too, can convincingly take on various roles.

Like actors, teachers can hone their skills in the use of props, can make better use of subject-matter-related humor (e.g., pun, short story, joke, riddle), and can create attention-getting suspense and surprise. Not only *can* teachers use all of these acting-related tools; we argue that they *must* use these tools. These tools, in conjunction with the educators' top-tray tools, can help teachers deliver their message more effectively.

ACTING SKILLS, TEACHER ENTHUSIASM, AND STUDENT ACHIEVEMENT

With the introduction of the toolbox analogy and the tools (skills) contained within the toolbox, it is now time to expand the "Teacher Enthusiasm and Student Achievement" diagram presented in chapter 1. We can now add the specific acting/teaching skills contained within the toolbox to the diagram, as in figure 2.2.

The educational foundations for teachers' use of acting skills is laid in chapter 3, followed by a series of chapters introducing specific acting skills and relating how they can, and do, apply to the classroom.

ENTHUSIASM RATING CHART

How enthusiastic are you in the classroom? A rough indication of your enthusiasm level can be estimated by referring to the "Enthusiasm Rating Chart" by Collins (1981), reproduced in figure 2.3. One could simply examine the categories, for example, Vocal Delivery through Overall Energy Level, and the descriptors that are used to rate oneself as Low, Medium, or High, in order to get a rough estimate of one's enthusiasm. Although it is a bit more threatening, one could also ask a colleague to peer-review a class using this same chart as a basis for data collection. Surely repeated measurements, across several classes, should be taken before any definitive judgment is made.

Is it OK for teachers to incorporate the characteristics typified by the descriptors under the High column? Is it OK for teachers to move from excited speech to a whisper, to use demonstrative gestures, to change facial expression suddenly, to use unpredictable body movements? We argue, "Yes!" The remaining chapters in this book address how many of these characteristics of enthusiastic teachers can be enhanced.

SUMMARY

Clearly, teachers' perceived enthusiasm can be enhanced through the judicious use of the skills outlined in this chapter, which until now may have been seen only as relating to the acting world. These skills, whether used by teachers or actors, are simply a means to an end. They are the tools of one's craft. The more of these acting tools that teachers have at their disposal, and the better they are able to use them, the more effective these teachers will be in the classroom.

Figure 2.2
Acting Skills, Teacher Enthusiasm, and Student Achievement

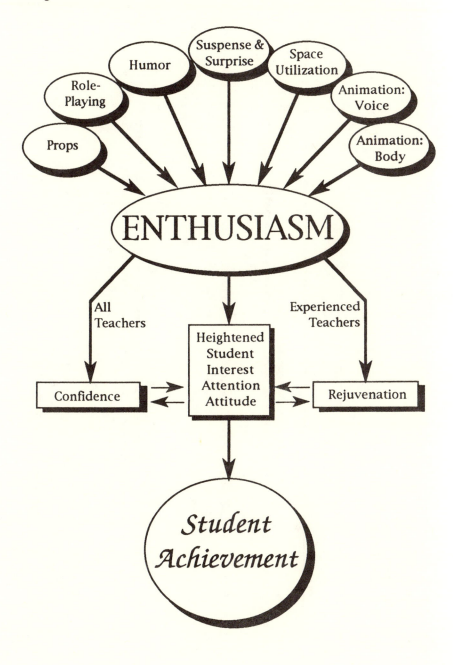

Figure 2.3
Enthusiasm Rating Chart

CATEGORIES	LOW	MEDIUM	HIGH
1. Vocal Delivery	Monotone, minimum inflections, little variation in speech; poor articulation.	Pleasant variations in pitch, volume, and speed; good articulation.	Great and sudden changes from rapid, excited speech to a whisper; varied tone and pitch.
2. Eyes	Looked dull or bored; seldom opened eyes wide or raised eyebrows; avoids eye contact; often maintains a blank stare.	Appeared interested; occasionally lighting up, shining, opening wide.	Characterized as dancing, snapping, shining, lighting up, opening wide, eyebrows raised; maintains eye contact.
3. Gestures	Seldom moved arms out toward person or object; never used sweeping movements; kept arms at side or folded, rigid.	Often pointed; occasional sweeping motion using body, head, arms, hands, and face; maintained steady pace of gesturing.	Quick and demonstrative movements of body, head, arms, hands, and face.
4. Body Movements	Seldom moved from one spot, or from sitting to standing position; sometimes "paces" nervously.	Moved freely, slowly, and steadily.	Large body movements, swung around, walked rapidly, changed pace; unpredictable and energetic; natural body movements.

Figure 2.3 (continued)

CATEGORIES	LOW	MEDIUM	HIGH
5. Facial Expression	Appeared deadpan, expressionless or frowned; little smiling; lips closed.	Agreeable; smiled frequently; looked pleased, happy, or sad if situation called for.	Appeared vibrant, demonstrative; showed many expressions; broad smile; quick changes in expression.
6. Word Selection	Mostly nouns, few adjectives; simple or trite expressions.	Some descriptors or adjectives or repetition of the same ones.	Highly descriptive, many adjectives, great variety.
7. Acceptance of Ideas & Feelings	Little indication of acceptance or encouragement; may ignore students' feelings or ideas.	Accepted ideas and feelings; praised or clarified; some variations in response.	Quick to accept, praise, encourage, or clarify; many variations in response.
8. Overall Energy Level	Lethargic; appears inactive, dull or sluggish.	Appeared energetic and demonstrative sometimes, but mostly maintained an even level.	Exuberant; high degree of energy and vitality; highly demonstrative.

Chart courtesy of Mary Lynn Collins. (Adapted from *Practical Applications of Research, PHI DELTA KAPPA Newsletter*, June 1981.)

CHAPTER 3

EDUCATIONAL FOUNDATIONS FOR TEACHERS AS ACTORS

All the world's a stage,
And all the men and women merely players:
They have their exits and their entrances;
And one man in his time plays many parts.
                        —Shakespeare, *As You Like It*

INTRODUCTION

Although, as Rubin (1985) argues, all the world may *not* be a stage, acting is part and parcel of everyday life. Everyone plays a role, in fact, many roles: parent, colleague, coach, neighbor, friend, and teacher. Acting, then, for most of us, is not used to deceive; it is used to stimulate and convince.

Although many readers may be more interested in the how-to chapters to come, little of what follows would be of any use to educators if it were not based upon firm pedagogical grounds. Educators are, and should be, held accountable for what they do in today's classrooms. Being accountable means, at a bare minimum, understanding *why* one uses the teaching strategies one does.

Teachers, like other professionals, have access to a unique body of knowledge they draw upon in order to do their job. It is not good enough simply to use teaching techniques that work, one must also know *why* they work. Without understanding *why*, teachers stop being professionals, and teaching stops being a profession. This chapter is designed to review the educational foundations for the use of theatrical devices as teaching strategies.

When we think of theater, we think of acting and the goals of entertainment, whereas in our classrooms we think of teaching and the goal of informing. Because these two goals are often deemed incompatible, entertainment has been a dirty word to many instructors. More than once we have overheard a teacher, with a scowling face (figure 3.1), proclaim in class with some vehemence: "I'm paid to educate you, not entertain you." The fact these instructors fail to realize is that if they expect to educate their students, they must, in some form or another, first attract and hold their attention—just as an actor must do.

Figure 3.1
Scowling Face

Drawing courtesy of Mark Fisher.

EDUCATIONAL FOUNDATIONS FOR TEACHERS AS ACTORS: THEORISTS SPEAK

All teachers want their students to value what is taught. According to the taxonomy for the affective domain of learning (Krathwohl, Bloom, and Masia 1956), *receiving* is a prerequisite to *valuing*. Therefore, before students can possibly have a commitment to something (value it), they must first be willing to give controlled or selected attention to it, both physically and mentally.

If we expect students to absorb the material presented and discussed in class, we must cultivate their attention by offering the material in an interesting and captivating way. This is, essentially, what we mean by entertainment. Entertainment is a means to an end.

According to Jerome Bruner, a cognitive psychologist whose work is well known, such attention and interest can be generated through the use of "dramatizing devices," including the development of a dramatic personality on the part of the teacher (1960, 82–83). These strategies support his fourth major theme in *The Process of Education* (1960), the consideration of how students' interest in learning can be stimulated.

Other cognitive psychologists use a three-part Information Processing Model to depict how learners recognize, transform, store, and retrieve information. The three parts include: Sensory Register, Short-term (working) Memory, and Long-term Memory. Simply put, information available in the sensory register will be lost if not *attended to*! It follows, then, that information (e.g., concepts, principles) will not reach one's short-term or long-term memory unless *attended to*. "Therefore, the first thing a successful teacher must do is to get students to attend to important material" (Dembo 1988, 343). Getting students to focus their attention on the task at hand is a necessary, if not sufficient, condition for learning to take place.

Similarly, Albert Bandura (1986), a name synonymous with the study of modeling, notes that securing students' attention is first among four important elements involved in observational learning. Whether one is demonstrating a process in a chemistry lab, elaborating upon a Shakespearian play in a literature class, or showing the contrast between the letters "b" and "d" in a first-grade classroom, little or no learning will take place unless the teacher is able to hold students' attention.

For youngsters, natural attention-getters (and holders) are those persons whom they perceive to be attractive, popular, successful, and interesting. We should not be surprised, then, at the ease with which film stars, rock stars, and sports figures appear to command the attention of young people by their very presence. These stars are effective models because they are able to secure the first element of observational learning — attention. Hence the "big bucks" they are paid to endorse products from sneakers to stereos.

How are educators to compete with such natural attention-getters? For those teachers who are not startlingly good looking or who may be trying to teach the Crimean War in history the day after Duke has won the NCAA championship, is there hope? Yes, there is! Effective entertainment skills can be the great equalizer as teachers compete for getting (and holding) students' attention.

Clearly, the theorists offer sound educational foundations for teachers' use of acting skills as an enthusiasm-generating strategy to secure, as well as to hold, students' attention. No other single strategy seems to have the potential for generating perceived teacher enthusiasm — a characteristic shown to be associated with teacher effectiveness and student achievement.

EDUCATIONAL FOUNDATIONS FOR TEACHERS AS ACTORS: PRACTITIONERS SPEAK

Practitioners, in particular award-winning teachers, concur. In the research conducted prior to writing this book, we contacted award-winning professors in various disciplines and asked them to comment on their use of acting skills in the classroom. Their testimonials, which are included in Appendix II: Testimonials from Award-Winning Professors, testify to the need for teachers to incorporate acting skills in their teaching.

An English teacher agrees that acting skills "can be useful in engaging students in the course and focusing their attention on the major ideas or problems of a discipline" (Carroll, testimony 3). Another English teacher, with twenty years of experience, readily attests to the usefulness of acting skills as an "aid in maintaining both the vibrancy and quality of learning" (Harrison, testimony 7).

A biology teacher, although admitting that she has had no formal training in acting techniques, has "become increasingly aware of their [acting skills] importance to the quality and effectiveness" of her teaching (Grimnes, testimony 5). Another biology teacher claims that "good teaching sweeps people away and involves them in the mood of the acting production. It is the ability to involve an audience that a teacher must master if he/she is to be completely successful in teaching" (Light, testimony 9).

An instructor of theater and dance writes that acting skills "will help a teacher create classes with drama: classes that generate interest, sustain suspense, and leave students with a feeling that something important has been achieved" (Hall, testimony 6). According to a philosophy teacher, "students considering secondary-school teaching need to become very outgoing and spontaneous in their delivery. While instruction is never coextensive with entertainment, nonetheless to learn how to work an audience should not be downplayed" (Lisska, testimony 10).

The world of drama pervades a history teacher's comments when he says that he has spent a decade learning his craft "in an environment conducive to the development of educational acting skills and the awareness of the classroom as a stage upon which the instructor may combine aspects of the lecturer and the performer" (Mahoney, testimony 11). A psychology instructor, although admitting that his acting experience outside of the classroom has been limited, has "learned how to act, and how to teach, on the same stage." His use of acting skills has not limited his responsibility to teach content: "they simply enhance the content and make it a part of the student's reality" (McBrayer, testimony 12).

A marketing teacher acknowledges the importance of teaching up-to-date, well-organized material. The real challenge, she argues, is to "teach the material each time as if it's the first time. Every 'performance' must retain the excitement of opening night. For every member of the audience, after all, it is just that" (Rogers, testimony 14). In a response typical of those received from our award-winning teachers, a political science instructor starts off her testimony with, "I never thought of myself as an actor" (Steuernagel, testimony 18), and then goes on to enumerate teaching techniques that she believes she shares with fellow performers.

Our testimonials support Kelly and Kelly's (1982) interviews with, and observations of, award-winning teachers. Among other common elements, the teachers compared their teaching to a theatrical performance. Effective basic-education and higher-education teachers reported that they "come alive" when they step in front of the class. At this point they feel they are on stage. When educators take on the teacher role, they are able to speak with a sense of confidence and enthusiasm that energizes both themselves and their students.

In a recent special issue of *Communication Education*, writers offered a series of "docustories" celebrating situations when teaching actually "worked." Immediately following these stories, four guest authors critiqued the stories attempting to analyze common elements. One such element was performance. Conquergood (1993, 338) sees successful teaching as a shift from informative to performative. Sprague (1993, 356) cites the common element of "teaching as assisted performance." Strine (1993, 374) sees teaching as crossing "comfort zones" where lessons are learned from performing.

Wulff (1993), an associate director of a center for instructional development, acknowledges how the various contributors' stories have influenced him. When faculty visiting his center ask, "What makes you successful in helping faculty with their teaching," his first inclination is to enumerate a series of reasons. Instead, now he says, "Let me tell you a story. . . ." Storytelling is probably the oldest, and most enduring, of the performing arts!

Worldwide, the message — the evidence — is the same. The dramatic style of teachers in many cultures emerges as one of the highest correlates of teacher effectiveness (Sallinen-Kuparinen et al. 1987). In Australia, for example, Holloway, Abbott-Chapman, and Hughes (1992) report that a common element among effective teachers was demonstrated through their enthusiastic — to the point of being highly dramatic — presentation of subject matter.

Successful practitioners, everywhere, in every discipline, and at every grade level, agree: there is an educational foundation for using acting skills in the classroom.

THE PROFESSION'S RESPONSE; OR LACK THEREOF

Although there are strong educational foundations for teachers' use of acting skills in today's classrooms, too few teachers are prepared to do so. It is not their fault. They should not be blamed because they have not been trained. Today's teachers have not, by and large, had acting-skills training — whether in their current inservice programs or in their previous teacher training. Tomorrow's teachers, those still in training, fare no better.

For instance, in Australia, a bulletin board announcement at the University of Melbourne's School of Education shows that teachers-in-training themselves recognize the connection between drama (acting skills) and effective teaching. The announcement, "Using Drama Techniques Across the Curriculum," reads:

Free up your teaching styles! Move away from chalk and talk! Drama is a powerful teaching strategy in any and all subject areas. Students will be enthused by experiential learning and your lessons will become more dynamic and interesting.

The three students advertising this non-credit elective, designed for non-drama method students, apparently felt the topic was not being stressed enough in their formal teacher training, and therefore they were going to do something about it.

Travers (1979, 16) wrote that the process of making your teacher-self "has been neglected by schools of education not because the matter seemed unimportant, but because the difficulties of providing training seemed insuperable." More than a decade later the task may be daunting but perhaps even more necessary. Teacher-training programs, whether at home or abroad, seem to overlook two crucial areas of skill development associated with making your teacher-self: speech communication and drama.

The first area overlooked in helping teachers develop their teacher-self is speech communication. Although not the specific focus of this book, many speech communication skills parallel those found useful in drama: animated voice, animated body, space utilization. It is astonishing that education majors—past and present—typically are required to take only one speech course, usually the same course that students majoring in agriculture, engineering, and liberal arts schedule. One would think that potential teachers, being prepared for a field so reliant upon speaking, would be required to schedule more than one speech course. Such is not the case.

Part of the reluctance of schools of education to incorporate more speech communication courses in their teacher education programs may spring from the attitude of educators (professors) themselves. In what could be viewed as an insult, if it were not so true, Nussbaum (1992, 177) comments: "Communication scholars have at least one advantage over education scholars: we read their literature. A quick look at the references of communication education articles indicates that our literature is influenced by the research findings in education. Education research rarely mentions any result from the communication discipline."

A concrete example of Nussbaum's damning assertion that educators ignore relevant topics in speech communication is the fact that the prestigious School of Education at the University of Melbourne recently canceled its education library subscription to *Communication Education*, the official journal for the Speech Communication Association. An inquiry to the head librarian revealed that she was instructed to cancel those journals used infrequently by faculty and students. Could it be that educators judge speech communication to be of little value in teaching? We hope not.

The second overlooked skill necessary to develop one's teacher-self is drama. The situation for preservice teachers is even worse when it comes to their receiving training in drama than it is in the area of speech communication. Typically, education majors are required to schedule no acting or drama courses. Yet Hanning (1984, 33) claims that teachers regularly "must give a performance, of sorts, in order to communicate effectively with students." Where, then, are teachers supposed to learn how to perform?

Why the reluctance to incorporate speech communication and acting skill development in yesterday's, as well as today's, education training? The answer is fear! It has been our experience that methods teachers in higher education (one of the authors of this book was a "methods teacher"), those who teach preservice teachers how to teach, are uncomfortable at best, and downright scared at worst, of anything that has to do with speech communication. Timpson (1982, 4) claims that "while professors of education will lecture about the components and varieties of effective instruction, they do little to assist teachers in developing anything beyond an awareness of ideals. There is, in other words, no practical training in this area."

This "fear" of speech communication *and* drama (acting skills) carries over to building administrators, for example, principals, in basic education—the very people who plan and sometimes themselves conduct inservice programs. What are we to do?

Some teacher-training institutions have tried to address this unmet need, although it typically occurs only if the faculty has someone on board who is comfortable with the field of drama. Rarely is such a course recommended across the board by a curriculum committee. Robert Keiper (1991), a professor with a drama background, has created such a course as part of his school's teacher-education program at Western Washington University. His two-credit pilot version of the course, with an enrollment cap of thirty, had over seventy undergraduate and graduate students and inservice teachers attempting to sign up for it the first day.

Unfortunately little help can be expected from educational psychology texts, even though such resources are supposed to present the best application of psychology to educational settings. For instance, with regard to the acting skill of humor, in spite of the fact that a number of best-selling introductory textbooks in educational psychology "employ humorous cartoons and illustrations, apparently to gain and maintain student interest and attention to make educational points more effectively, none of these texts examines the place of humor in teaching" (Bryant et al. 1980, 512–13). An examination by the authors of more current educational psychology textbooks (e.g., Glover and Bruning 1990; Woolfolk 1993) reveals that Bryant's 1980 observations are still true.

Even more distressing is the fact that if you were planning a search strategy of ERIC (Educational Resources Information Center) by using the *Thesaurus of ERIC Descriptors*, you would come up empty-handed. "Entertainment" is not one of its descriptors. You would have better luck accessing ERIC using CD-ROM, where you would find approximately three-hundred *Current Index to Journals in Education* (*CIJE*) and *Resources in Education* (*RIE*) citations (1/83–9/90) where the term "entertainment" appears in a title and/or abstract.

THE MASTER'S VOICE

For further discussion of the concepts and skills presented in this chapter, read the following paragraphs in Appendix II: Testimonials from Award-Winning College Professors: Baleja, 2; Borecky, 1, 5; Carroll, 1; Harrison, 1, 2; Lavin and Lewis, 2–8, 19–21; McBrayer, 6; Rogers, 1, 4; Selco, 2–9; Steuernagel, 1.

y people who plan and sometimes themselves conduct inservice
grams. What are we to do?
Some teacher-training institutions have tried to address this unmet need,
ough it typically occurs only if the faculty has someone on board who
comfortable with the field of drama. Rarely is such a course
ommended across the board by a curriculum committee. Robert Keiper
91), a professor with a drama background, has created such a course as
t of his school's teacher-education program at Western Washington
iversity. His two-credit pilot version of the course, with an enrollment
of thirty, had over seventy undergraduate and graduate students and
ervice teachers attempting to sign up for it the first day.
Unfortunately little help can be expected from educational psychology
ts, even though such resources are supposed to present the best
plication of psychology to educational settings. For instance, with regard
the acting skill of humor, in spite of the fact that a number of best-selling
roductory textbooks in educational psychology "employ humorous
toons and illustrations, apparently to gain and maintain student interest
d attention to make educational points more effectively, none of these
ts examines the place of humor in teaching" (Bryant et al. 1980, 512–13).
examination by the authors of more current educational psychology
tbooks (e.g., Glover and Bruning 1990; Woolfolk 1993) reveals that
yant's 1980 observations are still true.
Even more distressing is the fact that if you were planning a search
ategy of ERIC (Educational Resources Information Center) by using the
esaurus of ERIC Descriptors, you would come up empty-handed.
itertainment" is not one of its descriptors. You would have better luck
:essing ERIC using CD-ROM, where you would find approximately three-
ndred *Current Index to Journals in Education* (*CIJE*) and *Resources in
ucation* (*RIE*) citations (1/83–9/90) where the term "entertainment" appears
a title and/or abstract.

IE MASTER'S VOICE

For further discussion of the concepts and skills presented in this chapter,
d the following paragraphs in Appendix II: Testimonials from Award-
inning College Professors: Baleja, 2; Borecky, 1, 5; Carroll, 1; Harrison, 1,
Lavin and Lewis, 2–8, 19–21; McBrayer, 6; Rogers, 1, 4; Selco, 2–9;
:uernagel, 1.

The world of drama pervades a history teacher's comments when he says that he has spent a decade learning his craft "in an environment conducive to the development of educational acting skills and the awareness of the classroom as a stage upon which the instructor may combine aspects of the lecturer and the performer" (Mahoney, testimony 11). A psychology instructor, although admitting that his acting experience outside of the classroom has been limited, has "learned how to act, and how to teach, on the same stage." His use of acting skills has not limited his responsibility to teach content: "they simply enhance the content and make it a part of the student's reality" (McBrayer, testimony 12).

A marketing teacher acknowledges the importance of teaching up-to-date, well-organized material. The real challenge, she argues, is to "teach the material each time as if it's the first time. Every 'performance' must retain the excitement of opening night. For every member of the audience, after all, it is just that" (Rogers, testimony 14). In a response typical of those received from our award-winning teachers, a political science instructor starts off her testimony with, "I never thought of myself as an actor" (Steuernagel, testimony 18), and then goes on to enumerate teaching techniques that she believes she shares with fellow performers.

Our testimonials support Kelly and Kelly's (1982) interviews with, and observations of, award-winning teachers. Among other common elements, the teachers compared their teaching to a theatrical performance. Effective basic-education and higher-education teachers reported that they "come alive" when they step in front of the class. At this point they feel they are on stage. When educators take on the teacher role, they are able to speak with a sense of confidence and enthusiasm that energizes both themselves and their students.

In a recent special issue of *Communication Education*, writers offered a series of "docustories" celebrating situations when teaching actually "worked." Immediately following these stories, four guest authors critiqued the stories attempting to analyze common elements. One such element was performance. Conquergood (1993, 338) sees successful teaching as a shift from informative to performative. Sprague (1993, 356) cites the common element of "teaching as assisted performance." Strine (1993, 374) sees teaching as crossing "comfort zones" where lessons are learned from performing.

Wulff (1993), an associate director of a center for instructional development, acknowledges how the various contributors' stories have influenced him. When faculty visiting his center ask, "What makes you successful in helping faculty with their teaching," his first inclination is to enumerate a series of reasons. Instead, now he says, "Let me tell you a story. . . ." Storytelling is probably the oldest, and most enduring, of the performing arts!

Worldwide, the message—the evidence—is the same. The dramatic style of teachers in many cultures emerges as one of the highest correlates of teacher effectiveness (Sallinen-Kuparinen et al. 1987). In Australia, for example, Holloway, Abbott-Chapman, and Hughes (1992) report that a common element among effective teachers was demonstrated through their enthusiastic—to the point of being highly dramatic—presentation of subject matter.

Successful practitioners, everywhere, in every discipline, and at every grade level, agree: there is an educational foundation for using acting skills in the classroom.

THE PROFESSION'S RESPONSE; OR LACK THEREOF

Although there are strong educational foundations for teachers' use of acting skills in today's classrooms, too few teachers are prepared to do so. It is not their fault. They should not be blamed because they have not been trained. Today's teachers have not, by and large, had acting-skills training—whether in their current inservice programs or in their previous teacher training. Tomorrow's teachers, those still in training, fare no better.

For instance, in Australia, a bulletin board announcement at the University of Melbourne's School of Education shows that teachers-in-training themselves recognize the connection between drama (acting skills) and effective teaching. The announcement, "Using Drama Techniques Across the Curriculum," reads:

Free up your teaching styles! Move away from chalk and talk! Drama is a powerful teaching strategy in any and all subject areas. Students will be enthused by experiential learning and your lessons will become more dynamic and interesting.

The three students advertising this non-credit elective, designed for non-drama method students, apparently felt the topic was not being stressed enough in their formal teacher training, and therefore they were going to do something about it.

Travers (1979, 16) wrote that the process of making your teacher-self "has been neglected by schools of education not because the matter seemed unimportant, but because the difficulties of providing training seemed insuperable." More than a decade later the task may be daunting but perhaps even more necessary. Teacher-training programs, whether at home or abroad, seem to overlook two crucial areas of skill development associated with making your teacher-self: speech communication and drama.

The first area overlooked in helping teachers develop their teacher-self is speech communication. Although not the specific focus of this book, many

speech communication skills parallel those found useful in drama: a voice, animated body, space utilization. It is astonishing that ed majors—past and present—typically are required to take only on course, usually the same course that students majoring in agr engineering, and liberal arts schedule. One would think that teachers, being prepared for a field so reliant upon speaking, w required to schedule more than one speech course. Such is not th

Part of the reluctance of schools of education to incorporate mor communication courses in their teacher education programs may spr the attitude of educators (professors) themselves. In what could b as an insult, if it were not so true, Nussbaum (1992, 177) cc "Communication scholars have at least one advantage over e scholars: we read their literature. A quick look at the refer communication education articles indicates that our literature is in by the research findings in education. Education research rarely any result from the communication discipline."

A concrete example of Nussbaum's damning assertion that ignore relevant topics in speech communication is the fact prestigious School of Education at the University of Melbourne canceled its education library subscription to *Communication Edu* official journal for the Speech Communication Association. An the head librarian revealed that she was instructed to cancel thos used infrequently by faculty and students. Could it be that educa speech communication to be of little value in teaching? We hop

The second overlooked skill necessary to develop one's teach drama. The situation for preservice teachers is even worse whe to their receiving training in drama than it is in the area communication. Typically, education majors are required to sc acting or drama courses. Yet Hanning (1984, 33) claims tha regularly "must give a performance, of sorts, in order to con effectively with students." Where, then, are teachers supposed to to perform?

Why the reluctance to incorporate speech communication and development in yesterday's, as well as today's, education train answer is fear! It has been our experience that methods teacher education (one of the authors of this book was a "methods teac who teach preservice teachers how to teach, are uncomfortable a downright scared at worst, of anything that has to do wi communication. Timpson (1982, 4) claims that "while professors of will lecture about the components and varieties of effective instru do little to assist teachers in developing anything beyond an aw ideals. There is, in other words, no practical training in this are

This "fear" of speech communication *and* drama (acting skills) to building administrators, for example, principals, in basic educ

PART II

THE ACTING LESSONS

CHAPTER 4

ANIMATION:
BODY

Actions speak louder than words.
— Anonymous

INTRODUCTION

Actors and teachers alike have two sets of inherent tools for conveying ideas and information to audiences — their bodies and their voices. Both can be used to provide emphasis, distinguish among ideas, clarify and create connotative meanings, thus complementing the verbal component of the message.

Our attention to our physical behavior in the classroom is especially warranted in this latter part of the twentieth century as we deal with an audience attuned since birth to the visual rather than the aural medium. Many teachers have been heard to complain that television has had such an impact that students cannot seem to pay attention to material unless it is presented in a visually stimulating manner. That reality is dealt with in this book as a challenge for teacher action rather than a cause for hand-wringing.

VALUE OF MODERATE ANIMATION

As is obvious from what has been said in earlier chapters about the value of enthusiasm, this book takes the position that a teacher who is moderately animated while presenting material will be somewhat more successful in getting that material across to the students. In the specific case of physical animation, we are referring to the use of facial expression, gesture, posture, and movement as nonverbal forms of expression that are found in the teacher's toolbox to convey enthusiasm. These four expressive elements will be referred to throughout this chapter.

Numerous researchers have raised questions about the relative value of teacher animation. In doing so, they have devised various experimental formats, asking teachers to act in a particular way or to imitate certain movements. Other studies have simply worked from a phenomenological basis and have analyzed the natural characteristics and unplanned behaviors of successful teachers. In both cases, the conclusions are similar: a teacher's nonverbal expression is positively linked to instructional effectiveness as long as that expressiveness is perceived as natural and is not excessive to the point of distraction (Andersen and Withrow 1987).

This perspective echoes the lesson learned by actors that careful, subtle physical expression complements the playwright's words, while excess or unnatural movement "steals the show." The actor has also learned that while some physical expression can be definitively planned in advance, the best is that which spontaneously reflects the actor's perception of the feelings and meaning of the words spoken. Such expressiveness is triply beneficial for the teacher, since it not only complements meaning but also contributes to the teacher's confidence and to the students' motivation.

Specifically, research conducted by Justen (1984) demonstrated that people trained in comfortable, expressive, physical movement were people who were able to speak with more confidence, thus developing better control of the total communication situation. This would seem to indicate that teachers who try to be more expressive will develop a certain amount of self-confidence as a fringe benefit.

Finally, several researchers whose work was summarized by Andersen (1986) concluded that a teacher's physical expressiveness positively impacts the students' affective domain. That is, the more expressive teachers (within reasonable bounds of moderation) are better liked by their students. Thus the students are more motivated to learn.

So, we can see that, like actors, teachers should act with a moderate level of animation, as is appropriate to their own enjoyment of the subject matter and of the process of teaching and learning. Their reward will be enhanced instructional effectiveness due to their own increased confidence and their students' increased motivation.

PURPOSES SERVED BY PHYSICAL ANIMATION

When a teacher gestures, uses a variety of facial expressions, changes posture, and moves about the room, it is done in order to achieve one of several specific instructional purposes. Grant and Hennings (1971) defined those purposes as "Conducting, Acting and Wielding." This categorization is meant to include only those movements considered to be instructional rather than personal in nature ("personal" meaning such movements as smoothing the hair, stifling a sneeze, etc.).

Movements that have the purpose of conducting would include gestures, head nods, and so on, that encourage or organize student responses. The teacher's movements in this instance essentially regulate the pattern and direction of class conversation.

Acting movements are those that serve the more basic communication functions of amplifying and clarifying meaning. Included in this category would be a variety of facial expressions and descriptive gestures.

Wielding movements would include any use of the hands or body needed to deal with physical objects used to supplement the verbal message. Like actors, teachers could consider such objects "props." These are discussed in more depth elsewhere in this book.

Other scholars would, no doubt, add to this list of purposes served by animation. The one additional purpose mentioned in several instances is that of establishing a desired power relationship between teacher and students. That is, a particular movement or posture may be used to convey or reinforce the teacher as an "authority figure." Knapp's work (1971) went so far as to identify very specific power-related teacher behaviors, for example, standing with arms akimbo and squaring the shoulders. The point here is simply that while many teacher behaviors serve to fulfill very specific instructional goals related to the subject matter, other behaviors have the purpose of contributing to the teacher-student power relationship.

A fringe benefit of physical animation that some may consider among its purposes is that movement can help diminish a speaker's perceived nervousness. By gesturing or moving about the room, nervous energy is burned up in constructive ways. This may be especially beneficial to the beginning teacher or to anyone whose confidence is flagging.

RECOMMENDATIONS FOR PRODUCTIVE TEACHER ANIMATION

As we turn to actual recommendations growing out of the accumulated studies on teacher movement, we should again recall the specific categories of movement to be considered. The standard categories are: facial expression (with special emphasis on eye contact), gestures, posture, and overall movement.

Facial expression is a tool for all speakers that exemplifies the communication saw, "One cannot *not* communicate" — our faces always convey some message to our listeners. The catch is that we are not always aware of what that message might be. As teachers, we would do well to sensitize ourselves to our own expressions so that our faces can be assisting the teaching process, not hindering it. For instance, are we smiling and nodding to encourage only certain or almost all students in the class? Has a grimace crossed our face before a student has finished replying?

We should be especially sensitive to the way we communicate with our students with our eyes. Via eye contact, we provide encouragement to our students, maintain their attention, show interest and concern, signal to the students, and portray our own confidence. Listeners tend to be quite sensitive to the initiation of eye contact. So, by looking directly at a student whose interest appears to be wavering, we rekindle his or her attention. We might even use our eyes to convey that we want that student to respond to a question or to start taking notes. In other circumstances, our direct eye contact may be read as a statement of confidence and commitment. By looking directly at the students, we establish that we feel we have something important to say and trust the students to attend to it.

Too often, as we must juggle notes, props, student papers, and so on, we break that eye contact and thus momentarily sever the teacher-student bond. As Lowman (1984) points out, this is what actors call "losing the house" and is nearly always fatal to anyone trying to build a sustained positive relationship between speaker and listeners. Hence the recommendation to maintain positive eye contact with the students as much as possible is a suggestion for the good of one's entire career as a teacher.

In addition to nurturing a positive teacher-student relationship, eye contact opens the door to student learning. When the teacher holds the student visually, it is hard for the student not to listen to the teacher's words. Once a student looks away, intellectual involvement with the material has probably ceased (Penner 1984).

Gestures include a nearly limitless range of hand and arm movements. In earlier times, we would have found textbooks recommending that teachers, like all speakers, should specifically plan each and every gesture ahead of time. Those earlier textbooks would also have suggested that specific gestures would always be interpreted in very specific, predictable ways. Fortunately the theories underlying such assertions have long since been found to be faulty.

Instead of such prescriptive recommendations, we would suggest that the best gestures for a teacher to use are those which are natural, purposeful, and non-distracting. Our enthusiasm for the subject matter and for the teaching act will typically show itself in gestures that reinforce, emphasize, encourage, and clarify. These might include, but not be limited to, jabbing the air, pointing to students or objects, contrasting one hand motion with another, or sweeping the air like an orchestra conductor. Arnold (1990) reports that one award-winning professor was famous for his repertoire of football referee signals that he used during class discussions. These gestures, which might seem extreme to some, were well received by the students. They believed that by his going to such extremes, he showed the degree to which he cared about their learning and his willingness to work hard to make it happen.

Figure 4.1
Sweeping the Air with Hands

Drawing courtesy of Mark Fisher.

Fundamentally, gestures, such as sweeping the air with one's hands (figure 4.1), are good if they are positively communicative. That means that the gesture should complement the words spoken. The gesture may be a *descriptive* one which clarifies the physical properties of the subject being discussed; it may be an *emphatic* one which indicates the most important aspect of the words spoken; or it may be *signalic*, indicating something the listeners are to do relative to the words spoken.

Gestures and facial expressions constitute the bulk of the teacher's physical animation. However, to a certain extent, a teacher's enthusiasm should occasionally reveal itself in the form of posture changes and overall movement. The best teachers certainly are often described as being "unable to contain themselves" because they find the material so interesting and, in some cases, exciting. Teachers have been known to leap in the air, for instance. This last action is not necessarily recommended for all of us. But certainly, if we feel so moved by a student's response or by the subject matter itself, we should allow ourselves to show that in a physical manner.

Posture also should be considered when establishing particular teacher-student power relationships. Generally, a person who is standing while others are sitting is an individual with relatively more power. Therefore, if the teacher wants to assert power, it may be wise to stand; whereas, if the teacher wants to establish an equality of power, it may be wise to sit.

One special moment in every class period in which total movement can be especially influential is at the beginning. As every actor knows, it is important to make a meaningful entrance. The same import is attached to a teacher's entrance. By our pace and posture at that precise moment, we essentially set the tone for the rest of the class period. We communicate eagerness, anger, dread, confidence, enthusiasm, all in those few short strides from the doorway as the class begins. The recommendation here, as in the other areas of physical animation, is simply to be sensitive. Know what message your body may be conveying in those few moments, and ask yourself if that is your *intended* message for the class.

Note that all of the above recommendations are suggestions for behaviors that *may* be beneficial to the teacher aspiring to do a more successful job of holding the students' attention and motivating them. There are no hard-and-fast "rules," and every teacher's individuality will define his/her comfort with physical animation. But no one of us should dismiss active gesturing and expressiveness simply because it may make us a little uncomfortable initially. It is too valuable a tool to ignore.

BEHAVIORS TO AVOID

While there are no strict rules about what to do in terms of physical movement, there are a few strict rules regarding what *not* to do. Some of our physical behaviors, committed out of habit, may actually be interfering with our efforts to create a positive learning environment.

As Dolle and Willems (1984) have observed, we may inadvertently be sending contradictory messages — our words sending one message and our behaviors conveying an opposite view. For instance, the teacher asks a student to speak ("The class is interested in your ideas,") but then conspicuously checks the time ("Aren't you done, yet?") before the student has finished. The student receives a mixed message. The teacher's words expressed interest, yet his or her concurrent actions expressed disinterest. Typically, listeners put more faith in a speaker's nonverbal message than the verbal. Consequently, in our time-checking example, the students will have probably inferred that the teacher's interest in the student's response was not sincere. That is an interpretation from which the teacher-student relationship will be slow to recover.

In the same vein, teachers should not begin to walk (other than to write on the board) while a student is talking (Fisch 1991). In doing so, the teacher would be "walking on the other's line," to use theatrical parlance. As theatergoers, we may have seen a background actor commit such an error, and we called it upstaging. The problem is that the other listeners in the room will be attracted to the person in motion instead of to the person speaking. So when the teacher upstages the student, he/she is essentially stealing the attention that the student has earned by participating. That will annoy not just the student who is trying to speak but all of his/her friends in the room as well. Such alienation is definitely something we want to avoid in teaching.

Finally, a teacher should avoid any physical actions or behaviors that could be considered distracting. Pacing and coin-jingling are probably the two most common examples of this fault. Such behaviors serve none of the goals or purposes mentioned earlier and, by their repeated nature, only invite student mockery. Since the behaviors in this category are frequently subconscious habits, we may be unaware of doing them and of how annoying they have become for the students. It may be in our best interest occasionally to ask a trusted student if there is anything about our classroom behavior that could be perceived as nervous habit or distraction in general. Then, of course, work to replace that bad habit with more constructive, purposeful behaviors.

SUMMARY

A great Canadian professor, Richard Day of McMaster University, has been described in this fashion: "His performance is rivetting. . . . [H]e never stops moving, circling, stalking" (Johnson 1991). It is telling that the student commentator used a performance metaphor to describe Day's classroom animation. Reflected again is the concept that, to a certain extent, we teachers are performing artists. As such, it would behoove us to follow the actors' guidelines in regard to physical movement. We should allow ourselves to move enough to create character, convey meaning, share enthusiasm, and hold the listeners' attention, but not so much as to become a caricature.

THROUGH THE STUDENTS' EYES

When surveyed regarding the use of animation in body in the classroom, students offered real-life examples such as those that follow. Although each example refers to the use of animation in body in a particular subject area, the application to other disciplines is evident.

Talk about Gestures

Mr. S., my geography teacher, was very dramatic. He always used some interesting gyration of his body to emphasize a certain point that he wanted us to remember. Once he asked me a question about a geographical region and I told him that I didn't know the answer. He immediately threw his tie over his shoulder, opened his eyes so wide that they were as big as saucers, and then grasped his chest as if he were having a heart attack. I'll never forget the answer that I didn't know — it was "The Gateway to the West."

English with a Flair

My English composition teacher used gesture and facial expression as a communicative form. No message about our work or the principles we were studying was ever conveyed with words alone. Her approach led to a more comfortable attitude toward learning for everyone in the class.

Jump in the Boat

My college choir director always gestures to get us to sing louder, softer, more intensely, etc. He even went so far as to walk like he was following a boat down a river, then he acted like he jumped into it. This was to illustrate that we must follow the music and jump in when it's our turn. Don't wait for the boat, follow it.

Creepy Crawly

My biology teacher was trying to get us to understand how a paramecium moves. Words didn't seem to be getting the point across, so she used her own body to demonstrate — creeping along just like a paramecium.

THE MASTER'S VOICE

For further discussion of the concepts and skills presented in this chapter, read the following paragraphs in Appendix II: Testimonials from Award-Winning College Professors: Baleja, 3, 4; Grimnes, 1–3, 5; Light, 2; Rogers, 3; Rotkin, 5; Steuernagel, 3.

CHAPTER 5

ANIMATION:
VOICE

It is not enough to know what to say,
but it is necessary to know how to say it.
— Aristotle

INTRODUCTION

The voice is an especially personal element in anyone's expressive repertoire. It reflects our character, background, personality, and moods. Using the voice to create and modify meaning should occur in a completely natural fashion for the speaker, with the particular expression growing out of — not overlaid on — the speaker's internal understanding and feeling for the ideas expressed.

Considerable research has been undertaken in an effort to determine whether a teacher's vocal expressiveness influences student learning. Results have varied considerably. Two overall conclusions seem to be firm, however: 1) a moderately inexpressive voice will not hinder learning (Knapp 1976); and 2) a moderately expressive voice correlates with more significant learning (Richmond, Gorham, and McCroskey 1987). So good vocal expression being potentially advantageous, the voice is certainly a subject worthy of consideration for the aspiring teacher.

VOCAL FITNESS

Actors, appreciative of the voice's potential, work to keep their voices healthy and flexible so that they can be responsive to moderate changes in emotion. Some actors do daily vocal exercises, some take voice lessons, and still others simply treat their voices with care so that the vocal folds will not be strained. Regular general exercise to maintain an overall level of fitness, well-balanced diets, and avoidance of abusive practices such as smoking are the basics of a sensible approach to maintaining vocal strength and flexibility. Teachers, being equally dependent professionally on their voices, should exercise similar care. Specifically, if voices are to be healthy enough to achieve the projection and expressiveness necessary in the classroom, teachers should:

- practice deep diaphragmatic breathing
- maintain relaxed throat muscles
- drink plenty of water and fruit juices
- avoid smoking and inhaling others' smoke
- whisper when bothered by a sore throat.

Why is this so? What is it about the human voice that makes it such an important instrument for both actors and teachers?

VOCAL VARIATIONS – PARALANGUAGE

Paralanguage is a term for the conglomerate of vocal variations that accompany oral verbal expression. Specifically, the elements of vocal pitch, speech rate, volume, and tonal quality are voice characteristics that are all capable of significant variation within any one individual.

Each of us has a certain vocal character that is identifiable as our own. In fact, recent developments in forensic science verify that each human voice is unique, possessing a distinct combination of variations within the four vocal characteristics. No one uses only *one* pitch level, or degree of loudness or rate, of course. We might speak, for instance, an average of 175 words per minute, but that is not a constant speed. We may slow down to 100 words per minute when speaking about something very tragic or somber and speed up to 225 words per minute when sharing exciting news. It is the *pattern* of variations that is constant for an individual and thus makes that person's voice unique.

So each of us has a range of vocal variations comfortably within our own vocal repertoire. We use those variations consciously and subconsciously to provide shades of meaning to the words we speak. A relatively significant amount of variation in a teacher's paralanguage will convey the enthusiasm that is positively correlated with higher student evaluations of teachers (Murray 1985).

SPONTANEOUS VARIATIONS

Most variations are determined subconsciously. As noted earlier, our voices should be responsive to variations in our thoughts and feelings.

When conflict is building within the scene of a play, the actor does not need to be reminded to speak more loudly and with greater variations in pitch. That change in voice is going to happen as a direct result of the actor's sensitivity to the developing conflict—he/she will *feel* angry and tense, and thus the voice will *sound* angry and tense. Similarly, as a teacher is presenting material found to be personally fascinating, no thought needs to be given to the idea of speaking with a higher pitch level, a faster rate, and a louder volume. Those vocal variations will likely occur simply because the teacher is so caught up in the material and, having a healthy voice capable of responding to changing emotional states, will experience vocal changes that convey that fascination. This is what was meant earlier in referring to variations that grow out of an involvement in our thoughts.

As teachers facing the challenge of holding the attention of easily distracted young people, it is especially important that we allow ourselves to use as much of our natural range as possible to make our ideas captivating and their full connotative meaning clear. This is precisely what aspiring actors spend hours practicing—expanding their ability to use comfortably their full vocal range. We would do well to follow their example.

DELIBERATE VARIATIONS

In addition to these natural patterns of pitch, rate, volume, and quality changes, we may make some deliberate decisions in order to provide specific vocal emphasis to our ideas. Again, there is a parallel in acting, for the actor knows ahead of time that, during the performance, a particular inflection is going to be necessary to create a specific meaning at certain key points. Let us look at each of the four vocal characteristics to understand how and why such deliberate variations would be planned for the classroom.

Pitch

Pitch, the highness or lowness of the voice, has the capacity to reflect a great many emotions and connotations. Rising pitch at the end of a thought group, for instance, typically indicates incredulity or questioning. A lowered pitch, on the other hand, indicates finality or certainty. So, if I were explaining an assignment to a class and stated the due date in a relatively lower pitch, the class would likely interpret this as a firm deadline. For example, "The term papers are due *on or before the 24th*" (with the italicized words spoken in a lower pitch). If a class had become somewhat lax in their homework responsibilities, I might want to plan deliberately to speak about the next assignment with such firmness and thus plan a particular pitch variation.

In a more routine vein, Andersen (1986) points out that pitch changes typically are perceived as signals indicating whose turn it is to speak – the teacher's or the students'. So pitch changes can be deliberately used both to convey feelings and to manage the classroom conversation flow.

Volume

Volume changes can be used similarly to convey a particular urgency or commitment about a statement. It is the *change* in volume that calls attention to the accompanying thought, not the volume level per se. Just being loud is not necessarily more beneficial than being quiet. As a famous commercial line notes, "If you want to get someone's attention, whisper" (figure 5.1). By purposely changing volume – either by speaking louder or softer – a teacher, like a good actor, focuses the listeners' attention on the point thus spoken. You might want to plan to change volume deliberately to convey a particularly suspenseful moment in a history lesson or an especially dynamic point in a science experiment.

In addition to considering volume changes, we should note that an adequate general volume is a fundamental necessity for both the actor and the teacher. Especially since a reasonably strong voice is perceived as conveying confidence, self-assurance, and control (Anderson 1977), it is a tool particularly beneficial to the beginning teacher. The general guideline is that, except in cases of confidentiality or emphasis as noted above, a sufficient volume should be maintained so as to make the speaker heard from anywhere in the room.

Quality

Voice quality is achieved as the result of our typical resonance and pattern of vocal fold movement. Frequent examples are breathiness, raspiness, stridency, nasality, and mellowness. Again, each one of us has a recognizable personal quality most of the time but may achieve variations in response to changing emotions or the need to convey a specific feeling. Generally speaking, we as teachers should try to maintain a pleasant quality devoid of any annoying effects such as hypernasality or stridency. After all, students will be listening to that voice for hours on end!

Actors who find they have a tendency to produce an annoying vocal quality seek professional assistance from speech coaches in order to achieve a pleasant, unstrained voice. Likewise, teachers should listen to their voices

Figure 5.1
Teacher Whispering

Drawing courtesy of Mark Fisher.

on tape to determine if the quality is pleasant enough for sustained attention.

Assuming that the basic quality has no distracting elements, voices should be capable of occasional quality variations. A teacher of literature, for example, may need to produce a more resonant, almost stentorian, tone when reading from some of Poe's work or a more breathy tone to read from Dickinson. These variations are achieved by modifying the resonating cavities (mouth, nose, and pharynx) or by changing the muscle tension on the vocal folds. e. e. cummings' voice is famous for its high-pitched stridency. Yet, in performing public readings of his poetry, even cummings was able to temper that quality for more romantic phrases or for conveying less contentious ideas.

Rate

Rate, the final variable vocal characteristic, has arguably the greatest potential as an expressive tool for the actor and teacher. Rate can be varied either by changing the overall speech speed (words per minute), changing the duration of a single syllable or word, or by using pauses of various lengths.

Slower overall rate or duration might be purposefully selected when we need to be perceived as speaking more seriously or emphatically. On the other hand, we may deliberately speed up to convey enthusiasm, panic, or surprise. The actor will have considered the script and plotted specific rate changes to match the intended meaning of the lines. While the teacher may not make such definitive plans, some advance attention to the lesson plan to determine which points could be emphasized by a simple rate change is appropriate. In addition, the other common teaching situation calling for a change in overall rate is when providing clarification if a student or students have failed to understand a concept. In that case, a slow deliberate speed should be used while watching closely for feedback from the involved student(s). As with volume, it is the *change* in rate that catches the listener's attention and provides emphasis.

Sometimes the classroom message is delivered best by a well-placed pause between words. Actors have long used this technique. Perhaps the best known "pauser" in the entertainment industry is Paul Harvey who uses the pause to keep his radio audience in suspense waiting for the "rest of the story." Pauses do that—they build suspense. But in addition, the pause is a device for punctuating our thoughts by separating items in a list, setting off direct quotes, pointing to key words or phrases, and signaling a change in focus. Strategically placed pauses can sometimes have a more dramatic effect on listeners' attention and comprehension than words themselves. In fact, studies that have analyzed the effect of "teacher wait time" — the time following a question asked by the teacher — indicate that by carefully using pauses, we enhance the likelihood of students' learning (Tobin 1986).

Teacher speech rate also has been shown to have an indirect effect on student learning because of its effect on student attentiveness. Students are less likely to be noisy when the teacher speaks at a moderate pace than at either a noticeably fast or slow pace (Grobe et al. 1973). Since they are less noisy, they are more attentive and susceptible to learning.

So, while the teacher, like the actor, should have a healthy, flexibly expressive voice capable of adapting to changes in mental orientation, persons in both roles are well advised also to plan a few deliberate modifications in vocal pitch, rate, volume, and quality.

INFLUENCING CREDIBILITY

We have spoken about such changes as assisting clarity by placing emphasis and establishing relationships among ideas. But vocal expressiveness has another very important benefit to both the actor and the teacher: influencing credibility.

While research indicates no direct causal link between a speaker's vocal expressiveness and listeners' retention or comprehension of messages, there is evidence that the speaker's expression does influence his or her perceived credibility and that credibility subsequently does influence the listeners' comprehension and retention (Knapp 1971) (figure 5.2).

Figure 5.2
Causal Link

Expressive Voice → Speaker Credibility → Listener Comprehension

Such credibility is crucial to the success of both the actor and the teacher for both must be believable "characters" to the listeners. Although the communicative goal is not persuasion, credibility is still an issue. Theater critics, for instance, frequently refer to believability as a criterion for measuring the quality of an actor's portrayal — the audience must sense that they are listening to *Hamlet*, not Sir Laurence Olivier. Thus, in trying to develop the best combination of vocal cues, the actor is fixing on a manner of articulation that can be consistently sustained and will positively influence the listeners' perception of the speaker's credibility.

Teachers should also be cognizant of the need to establish credibility in the classroom. In order for students to be motivated to be attentive and purposeful, they must believe in the teacher's expertise, interest in the subject matter, and interest in them as students. That is credibility.

Therefore, the best kind of vocal expression is that which is natural, sounds unforced, and allows the teacher's true feelings about the subject matter and the learning process to be evident. This goal brings us back to an earlier point suggesting that a relatively relaxed physical state will allow the voice to reflect feelings and attitudes. When the students can pick up on subtle vocal suggestions—pitch, rate, volume, and quality changes that place emphasis—they will believe that the teacher is knowledgeable and sincere. Consequently, they will be likely to remain relatively attentive, thus enhancing the possibilities of learning.

Credibility, and thus overall impact, is also enhanced by the speaker's ability to maintain vocal control. That is, a controlled voice free of unplanned, nonproductive extremes conveys to the listeners that the speaker is in control of his or her emotions and in control of the situation. A good actor knows to engage in vocal warm-up exercises prior to a vocally demanding performance so that his or her voice will not squeak or become hoarse during the performance and betray a sense of uneasiness. If such a slip should occur, the listeners become overly conscious that they are watching a performance and the characters are not real. Thus the play's credibility is damaged.

Teachers, too, need to maintain control within the performance that is a class. Voices can contribute to the ability to maintain discipline in the class because the voice is a barometer of emotions. The students will immediately sense that the teacher is "losing it" if his or her voice breaks when telling someone to sit down, for example. The teacher who can dole out disciplinary instructions in a calm, firm voice is much more worthy of the students' respect than the one who shrieks in angry frustration. That respect will have beneficial ramifications for both the students' long-term learning as well as for the immediate quality of the classroom atmosphere. Such vocal control can be attained by performing warm-up exercises similar to those of the actor and/or by the simple process of taking a deep, cleansing breath before speaking in emotionally stressful circumstances such as disciplining (Anderson 1977). If the voice is in control, the teacher is in control.

SUMMARY

The human voice is an incredible resource of particularly remarkable value to teachers and actors. Like any resource, it must be treated with care in order to be appreciated fully. If teachers adopt vocal exercise regimens similar to those used by actors, they will find that their voices can be responsive to their feelings and that they can actually plan a few specific vocal variations to add clarity and emphasis to ideas. In addition, vocal expression contributes to the teacher's perceived credibility and control of the classroom situation, thus enhancing learning in the long term.

THROUGH THE STUDENTS' EYES

When surveyed regarding the use of voice animation in the classroom, students offered real-life examples such as those that follow. Although each example refers to vocal animation in a particular subject area, the application to other disciplines is evident.

The Three Witches

Mrs. H., my senior English teacher, would always read passages in different voices so that they fit the character she was quoting. For example, in the first scene of *Macbeth*, she read the lines in a witch-like voice. This made Shakespeare much more interesting and kept all of her students' attention. This, in turn, made it easier to grasp the concept of the play.

Huck and Jim

In English class we were reading the novel, *The Adventures of Huckleberry Finn*. My teacher thought that we would get more out of the book if he read a few significant passages out of it in the dialect it was meant to be. Well, he was right. With him reading in two different animated voices, one for Huck and one for Jim, I got a better perspective about the novel and enjoyed it more than I had expected to.

Achtung!

Our German teacher uses quite a variety of vocal expressions. When he wants to emphasize a particular point or a pronunciation we're having trouble with, he will say it louder than usual. He sometimes even makes a siren sound whenever we read or say something particularly important.

The Changing Times

My eleventh grade history teacher did something really creative with his voice that I thought helped me to learn about different time periods. When he was explaining a particular era in American history, he would use vocal expression that conveyed the sentiment most prevalent in that time—for instance, a happy, carefree expression for the 1920s and a sad voice for the 1930s.

Locker Room Follies

In high school gym class, we could get pretty rowdy in the locker room. Mr. W. would always tell us to be quiet, of course. But he didn't shout like most teachers do; he would say it real quietly. That really got our attention.

THE MASTER'S VOICE

For further discussion of the concepts and skills presented in this chapter, read the following paragraphs in Appendix II: Testimonials from Award-Winning College Professors: Baleja, 3, 4; Borecky, 4; Clough, 1, 2; Light, 2, 4; Rogers, 3; Rotkin, 1, 2, 5; Soenksen, 3, 5; Steuernagel, 3.

CHAPTER 6

CLASSROOM
SPACE

People like to be close enough to obtain warmth and comradeship, but far enough away to avoid pricking one another.

—Sommer

INTRODUCTION

Acting out a behavior causes the person doing it to develop the actual feeling conveyed by the acted behavior. For instance, if one is afraid and needs to feel more courageous, *acting* courageous would be a useful strategy that would actually cause the fear to abate somewhat.

Many times a teacher, particularly a beginning teacher, may feel uncomfortable in the classroom. Applying the above logic, forcing oneself to use the space of the classroom in a manner that *looks* comfortable would not only convey to students that the teacher *is* comfortable in that room but also would nurture an enhanced feeling of comfort within the teacher as well.

Thus we now turn to consideration of constructive, purposeful use of the classroom space as a facet of the teacher-role that contributes to teacher confidence and to student learning. Imaginative use of classroom space is, therefore, a means, not an end in itself—a means of achieving positive learning outcomes. As one "acts" the role of teacher, just as with any acting, the space of the stage/classroom, with its scenery and finite limits, must be seen as a potentially beneficial tool.

PROXEMICS

The study of the communicative effect of the physical space between interacting people is known as proxemics. We learn from that field of study that people consciously or subconsciously choose to be in a particular spot in relationship to others depending on their interpersonal relationship, the context of the communication, and their particular goals (Hall 1966). Our interpersonal locations are interpreted as sending messages – of coldness, interest, intimacy, danger, love, and so on – whether we consciously intend them to or not.

It is on the basis of these principles of proxemics, then, that the actor or director plans the placement of actors for each scene. In real interactions with others, of course, we do not *plan* each and every placement of ourselves, but the proxemic message is still present.

The teacher can apply proxemics in as deliberate a way as the actor does, by planning his/her placement during a class period. In addition, the teacher's awareness of the value of proxemic messages will allow relatively spontaneous decisions regarding where he/she should be in the classroom to convey a particular point. Let us turn to the specific applications of proxemics to the performance art of teaching.

SPACE AND ITS LIMITATIONS

As oral communicators, both actors and teachers can benefit from being observant of the effect of space on the impact of their communication. Since nonverbal elements are part of the message communicated (be it dialogue or lessons), actors and teachers must, for instance, consider how well the listeners can see and hear them when they speak. The physical nature of the rooms within which we all must work will vary in terms of such things as acoustics and sight lines, and those elements will, in turn, impact upon the listeners' ability to attend to our messages.

As Lowman (1984) points out, some classes are held in rooms where the acoustics are awful. Students may hear an echo in some rooms, and in others the teacher may be inaudible to all students beyond the fifth row of seats. However, most classrooms, like most theaters, have been designed with good acoustics. It is, nonetheless, an issue of space to which the teacher may need to be sensitive. Some teachers, for instance, are reported to have roped off the rear rows of seats because of poor acoustics (Lowman 1984).

The issue of sight lines should also occur to teachers, just as it does to actors and directors. The question in this instance is: from what point in the classroom (or on the stage) can I be seen by listeners seated at various points around the room? Being seen by the listeners is, after all, a prerequisite to being heeded. A director will work from the set designer's drawings which include sight lines to make decisions about where to place actors within the stage space (figure 6.1). Such decision-making is known as blocking.

While such artificially predetermined decisions may seem far better suited to the theater than the classroom, the basic principles upon which blocking is based certainly carry over to the classroom. A review of these basic principles is in order here.

Figure 6.1
Sight Lines

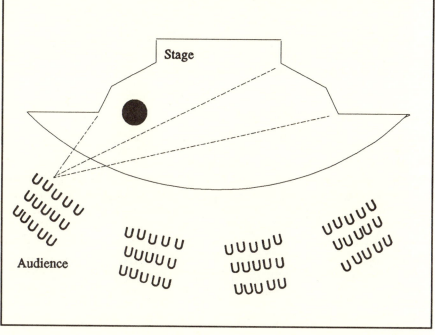

BLOCKING THE SCENE

A director or the actor involved must study the space available, the character's relationship to other characters on stage, and the character's specific motivation in order to determine the precise placement of the character within the stage space that would best convey that motivation and relationship to the audience. Placements must be compatible with established sight lines for the majority of the audience.

As the cast prepares for a performance, each piece of dialogue is thus blocked. During rehearsals, the blocking is reviewed and revised as needed to make sure its purpose is accomplished. Through rehearsing, the placement of the actors becomes firm and is ultimately perceived by the audience as integrated totally into the scene's creation of mood and idea.

The purpose of engaging in the tedious process of blocking is to place the actor in the precise spot on stage that will:

1. establish his/her relationship with the other characters on stage;
2. emphasize the point of the lines delivered from that spot; and
3. control and maintain the audience's attention.

Thus the actor's use of space is a nonverbal means of communicating.

Can a teacher do that same kind of purposeful planning of movement and placement within the classroom space? *Should* a teacher make such precise plans? Given the nature of the impact of space as a communicative message in any situation, the answer is a *qualified* "yes."

BLOCKING THE CLASS PERIOD

Movement around the classroom will be most effective if planned in conjunction with a thorough review of the material to be presented on a given day. Some portions of a math lesson, for instance, are going to demand that the teacher be near the chalkboard, while other portions allow more options in using the classroom space.

Whatever the case may be—whether a teacher has many or few constraints on how the classroom space can be used—the goals of selecting the best use of space are the same for the teacher as they are for the actor. The teacher should place him/herself in the classroom in such a way as to:

1. establish the desired relationship between teacher and students;
2. provide emphasis for the most important ideas of the lesson; and
3. maintain the students' attention.

If a teacher's material and style seem to result in a lecturing format in which many notes must be presented to the students, does that necessarily mean that the teacher must spend the whole class period by the chalkboard? The answer is no.

A teacher's awareness of the proxemic effect of free use of space by a lecturer necessitates occasionally breaking away from the podium and chalkboard. Pedagogically, such movement is beneficial in that it allows the teacher to be more physically expressive, to establish meaningful proximity with the students, and to create a confident, professional image.

The podium is especially problematic in that it can be perceived as a barrier insulating the teacher from the students. Since most of us want our students to perceive us as *not* wanting to be distant, we need to get out from behind the desk or podium. We can conceive of several ways to break away from the chalkboard or podium during the lecturing mode. Such a planned break would allow the teacher to be in closer proximity to the students, thus conveying a greater interest in their responses and allowing for more control of classroom behavior, if needed (Geske 1992).

The break from the chalkboard can be accomplished when using a lecture format, for example, by planning and preparing overhead transparencies or flip charts of the desired notes. A student seated near the projector or chart can turn pages as needed, while the teacher is free to place him/herself within the room where it makes the most sense for both holding the students' attention and emphasizing the key points of the material.

Another possibility would be to use poster boards placed strategically around the room in place of the chalkboard. The posters could be prepared in advance but revealed at the most appropriate moment or left with some blank spaces to be filled in as the teacher moved about the room.

Advance blocking of an *entire* class would, of course, be inappropriate since it would result in awkward movements and limit the spontaneity necessary for the learning process. But some consideration, in advance of the class meeting, of beneficial teacher and student placement during the lecture or discussion could be useful.

CLASSROOM SEATING

The classroom seating arrangement—a factor that both influences the students' attentiveness and constrains the teacher's use of space—deserves special attention as we consider the planned blocking of a class period. Teachers have long realized that students sitting in certain areas of the room tend to be more attentive and responsive than others. While this is due in part to the tendency of more communicative students to select seats within the teacher's direct line of sight, the seat a student happens to be in is also a factor that can cause slight modification of his/her pattern of responsiveness (Hurt, Scott, and McCroskey 1978). It would follow that if we want to encourage students to be more responsive, we can either move ourselves so that we will come within their direct line of sight or move the students, or both.

As we think about the possibilities of moving the teacher, the image of Professor Keating as played by Robin Williams in the film *Dead Poets' Society* (1989) comes to mind. Keating evidently was aware of the need to place himself in the most attention-getting position in the room, in spite of the constraints of the prep school's classroom. So we saw Keating in one memorable scene actually standing on the desk to deliver his lecture and, in another instance, kneeling down between rows of students so that they could huddle around him as he revealed an important insight about literature. While these situations may seem extreme, they illustrate the range of options available that a teacher may want to "block" ahead of time in order to increase student attentiveness and learning.

Moving the students, on the other hand, is a somewhat more complicated undertaking, not as open to extremes. There are so many more people to move, and the possibilities are finitely constrained by the size of the classroom and number and type of desks involved. With a reasonable number of students in a fair-sized classroom, for instance, student desks can be arranged in a circle in order to promote multi-channel communication (Billson and Tiberius 1991). Even the most inflexible of arrangements — chairs and desks bolted to the floor — can still allow some rearrangement of students, however. We should not be too quick to concede defeat.

One teacher dealing with this most inflexible of seating arrangements, for instance, developed a rotating seating chart. She had observed that certain seats in the room were "dead spots" because the students seated there had a poor view of the demonstration table at the front of the room. Certain other seats, however, were known to encourage the holders to be more attentive and responsive due to their bird's-eye view of the demonstration table. The teacher adjusted to this constraint by numbering the seats and establishing a regular rotation so that each student would move up one number each week of the course. Thus everyone had a turn at the "good seats."

Mentioning the table at the front of the room brings us to another important option for rearranging furniture to make best use of the classroom space. With the exception of lab rooms with demonstration tables needing certain gas and water hookups, most classrooms have a "front" only because that is where someone has arbitrarily placed the teacher's desk, wastebasket, flag, and so on. In other words, the "front" can be moved just by moving those accoutrements. By occasionally doing so, we change the students' visual focus during class and thus renew their attention.

In such typical straight-row classrooms, we would also have the option of simple rearrangement of students. Students can be moved in and out of the "prime seats" by a simple front-to-back periodic rotation. Another option would be to rearrange the student desks in some variation of small clusters (squares, parallel angles; figure 6.2). The advantage of doing so is greater student-student visibility (Walz 1986). Thus students can hear each other better and be reinforced by their peers' responses.

Figure 6.2
Seating Variations

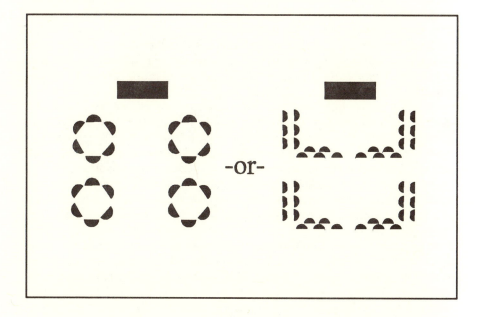

Student seats should be placed so as to give the teacher a great deal of space to move and simultaneously put the teacher in close proximity to as many of the learners as possible. Thus opportunities for creative use of space are enhanced, and it is easier to maintain attentiveness from *all* the students. In addition, as research has concluded, teachers are perceived more positively if they are occasionally within the student's personal space instead of maintaining a public distance.

To a certain extent then, teachers, like actors, can block their positions within the confines of the "scenery" (e.g., chalkboard, desks, walls) in order to enhance student attention, clarify focus, and establish intergroup relationships. Such blocking is done prior to the class by carefully considering the nature and substance of the material to be presented and both the limitations and creative possibilities afforded by the available classroom space.

SPONTANEOUS USE OF SPACE

Just as good actors can improvise on occasion, so good teachers can also make spontaneous decisions about where to place themselves, their students, or their materials within the classroom space. Such decisions grow out of the teacher's continual sensitivity to the students — their moods, levels of comprehension, and interests.

Recalling that the teacher's proximity to a student or students establishes the specific student-teacher relationship, we realize that there will be occasions when that relationship reflects a hierarchy of power, other times when a more caring relationship is indicated; and yet other times when the relationship is somewhere in between. Such variations cannot be blocked ahead of time.

Instead, as we are interacting with students — whether it be in a lecture, discussion, or practicum mode — we should be attentive to their feedback. One instructor who frequently has class in a large lecture hall reports, for instance, that students' postures and facial expressions often signal to him the need to come into their space to renew and refocus their attention on the material (Kurre 1993). Others, who more frequently use a class discussion format for teaching, may note that students' nonverbal behavior indicates when the teacher needs to come to that group and when to keep his/her distance.

The point is that in order to use classroom space most productively as a teaching tool, one must be comfortable enough in the space to move about it spontaneously as dictated by the material and the student responses. The teacher has to be able and willing on a moment's notice to pick the spot that will indicate the relationship between him/herself and the students and that will be most conducive to learning.

One could, for example, lean on the window sill, sit in a student desk, stand in the doorway, or walk slowly among the student desks. Each of these actions represents a break from the typical or expected teacher behavior of standing by the desk or podium — a break that could change the students' perception of the teacher's meaning and/or attitude.

For instance, in conducting a student discussion of literature, a teacher may convey an attitude of respecting and encouraging student opinion by sitting in a spare student desk instead of standing at the front of the room. Standing at the front, after all, reinforces the perception of the teacher as the person "in charge" of the class. Thus, if the teacher notes that the students seem reluctant to share ideas, it may be that a change in space relationship is needed. By moving to sit at eye level with the students, a different power relationship is indicated.

This type of relatively spontaneous change in the planned use of the classroom space is enabled by teacher sensitivity to the dynamics of the learning environment. As with any communicative event, the teaching-learning event must be planned carefully *but* with allowances for necessary adaptations to be made on the spot.

Spontaneity, though, can lead to some hair-raising experiences — literally. One of the authors, while speaking before a group of teachers at Darwin

Figure 6.3
Teacher on Table Close to Ceiling Fan

Drawing courtesy of Mark Fisher.

High School in Darwin, Australia, decided to emphasize a point by leaping onto one of the classroom tables. Although he assured himself that the table would hold his two-hundred pounds, he neglected to take into account his six-foot, two-inch height *and* the classroom's slowly turning ceiling fans! His head just missed those swirling blades (figure 6.3). It was almost an event everyone, *except* the author, would remember for a lifetime.

SUMMARY

In the theater, actors and directors consciously apply principles of proxemics (the study of interpersonal space) to determine the best placement for each of the characters within a scene. This is done to help the audience understand the playwright's point in the scene. The blocking of positions is planned and practiced well in advance of a performance, with some allowance for improvisational movement under certain circumstances.

Similarly, an effective teacher will consider, prior to a class meeting, the best placement of the people involved in the class — teacher and students — to enhance the likelihood of meaningful learning. This planning may result in the preparation of certain teaching aids, in the rearrangement of furniture or seat assignments, or in rehearsed movements within the classroom space available. In addition, the teacher is always prepared to modify such plans and spontaneously make decisions about his/her placement in the room in order to achieve the goals of:

1. establishing the nature of the teacher-student relationship;
2. emphasizing key points in the class material; and
3. maintaining student attention.

These have always been among the goals of all teachers, but we are all creatures of habit and may feel uncomfortable moving around a classroom in new ways. Just as an actor learns a part gradually, so a teacher should attempt to learn new approaches to using classroom space gradually, developing new strategies to enhance achievement of old goals.

Research conclusions unanimously confirm that teacher and student locations in a classroom affect their communication processes (Smith 1979). In teaching, as in acting, communication is, after all, the heart of the matter!

THROUGH THE STUDENTS' EYES

When surveyed regarding the use of space in the classroom, students offered real-life examples such as those that follow. Although each example refers to the use of space in a particular subject area, the application to other disciplines is evident.

Table Walking

One day, about five minutes after the students had filed into class, Mr. B. came running into the classroom and jumped onto the table. Talk about shock (surprise)! Our tables were in a circle, and he proceeded to walk around them explaining the rules of the "math game." He would walk around reciting a math sequence of operations and when and where he stopped (no one knew how long the math problem was [suspense]), that student would have to give the answer. The "game" definitely reinforced my math skills and yet entertained me at the same time.

Dealing with the Multitudes

My college Human Development class has four-hundred students in it. Ordinarily, there is very little class participation under these circumstances. But this professor is different. He comes down from the stage area and walks around the lecture hall. This gets people to participate and makes learning more fun.

An Upending Discussion

Our German teacher in high school was explaining different customs and behaviors typical of the country. When we got to the part about driving on the autobahn, he had us turn our desks upside down and line them up around the room to "create" an autobahn. Then he explained the German rules of the road.

Cornering the Problem

In math class at my high school, a teacher used the corner or corners of the room as a focal point to show the x, y, and z axes of three-dimensional space.

New Flooring

Frequently in my college French class, the professor will ask us to arrange our chairs in a U shape leaving wide-open floor space in the center. Then she spreads pictures around the floor pertinent to the day's lecture topic. That way, we can all see the pictures much more easily than if the same things were hung on a bulletin board.

THE MASTER'S VOICE

For further discussion of the concepts and skills presented in this chapter, read the following paragraphs in Appendix II: Testimonials from Award-Winning College Professors: Clough, 4; Grimnes, 1–3, 6; Mahoney, 3; McBrayer, 2; Steuernagel, 2–5.

CHAPTER 7

HUMOR

One of the most important qualities of a good teacher is humor.
— Highet

INTRODUCTION

As the story goes, Joe accompanied his friend to a joke-tellers meeting. At the well-attended gathering, members had such a large repertoire of jokes that they numbered each of them. Then, throughout the meeting, different members simply would stand, call out the number of a joke (e.g., #42, #89), and all in the audience would howl with laughter. Toward the end of the meeting, Joe asked if he could take a turn "telling a joke" — after all, it looked so easy. Joe stood, called out a number, and waited for an audience response. There was none. Joe's friend turned to him and said: "Well, some people can tell a joke, and some people can't."

Successful joke-teller or not, humor is everywhere. John F. Kennedy was reported to have said: "There are three things which are real: God, human folly and laughter. The first two are beyond our comprehension. So we must do what we can with the third" (Hunsaker 1988, 285). What can we do with humor?

On one hand, for both actors and teachers, humor should be the easiest skill area to address. Probably more has been written on the subject of humor than on any of the other acting/teaching skills highlighted in this book. On the other hand, humor is often seen as the most threatening of the skill areas. For teachers, humor may be even more threatening in that, for them, humor must serve a subject-related purpose, not simply entertain. Further, humor that "bombs" for an actor one night with one audience can be forgotten — a new audience will be in the theater tomorrow. For teachers, humor that "bombs" is remembered, not only by the students (audience) but by the teacher.

In spite of the anxiety, sometimes terror, that beginning users of humor might experience, it is worth the effort. "Humor, like sin, sun, and self-righteousness exists virtually everywhere people congregate" (Herbert 1991, 2). Humor holds great potential for positively impacting upon an audience, in the theater or in the classroom. People who possess a real sense of humor can take it as well as hand it out. This, too, is true whether one is on the stage or in the classroom.

HUMOR: ITS IMPACT UPON TEACHING

Javidi, Downs, and Nussbaum (1988) report that award-winning high school and mid-high school teachers use humor significantly more than their non-award-winning counterparts. These award-winning teachers "played off" the self, the students, others not in class, and the course materials in order to clarify course content. The humor to which we refer here is *constructive* humor — nonhostile humor directly related to the educational message — not just a funny joke. If we allow such humor to be a vital part of the lecture or demonstration, we will add a strategy to our repertoire that is sure to stimulate student attention. The bottom line is that "students learn more when they're having fun" (Sullivan 1992, 36).

We should remember that humor is one of the best ways teachers can develop a solid relationship with students. Humor helps teachers and students establish a rapport with one another — the ability to see the frailties of human nature, to be able to laugh at oneself and not take oneself too seriously. Victor Borge is reported to have said that "laughter is the shortest distance between two people." Laughter is one of the most visceral expressions of being entertained. Laughter also increases the student's ability to absorb knowledge. Nonhostile humor, directly related to the educational message, can also help make taboo subjects more approachable. It is a powerful way to reinforce learning.

Humor can take many forms, including that of playful exaggeration, an intentional expansion of emotional responses reinforced by gesture, posture, tone of voice, and role-playing. Such a form of acting, according to Starratt (1990, 19), "falls in between playing one's part with sincerity and playing an imposter or fraud." It recognizes that a play (or a class) "cannot tolerate relentless melodrama; neither can it sustain uninterrupted frivolity." This type of acting includes, among other exaggerated responses, "mock indignation ('How dare you, sir!'), mock surprise ('I never would have suspected!'), a playful moralizing ('That's what happens to little boys who disobey their mothers.') and stock rationalizations ('The devil made me do it!')." Observations about humor, no matter the form, reveal a concept that is multidimensional. It has intellectual, spiritual, and physical aspects (Goor 1989).

Humor invites students to take risks in the classroom because it softens the blow of failure. In *Dead Poets' Society* (1989), Mr. Keating, played by

Robin Williams, often uses humor to inspire his students to participate. One notable moment occurs when a student incorrectly answers a query about a certain poet. Williams makes the sound of a buzzer with his voice, giving the impression that the student is on a game show. The buzzing sound is followed with the line, "Incorrect (Charlie), but thank you for trying." This creates immediate laughter from the other students, as well as from Charlie. The students were discovering for the first time that learning and participating in class, even if the incorrect answer is given, can be exciting, fun, and safe.

> Humor helps to convert "Ha Ha" into "Aha!"
> — Herbert 1991

It soon becomes apparent when using humor that there are various categories of humor. Bryant, Comisky, and Zillmann classify humor (1979, 112–113), when used for pedagogical purposes, into the following categories: the joke ("a relatively short prose build-up followed by a punch line"), the riddle ("an information question with answer provided in a humorous punch line"), the pun ("structurally or phonetically similar words or phrases having two or more meanings"), the funny story ("a series of connecting events or the activities of a single incident as a tale"), and humorous comment ("brief statement with a humorous element which does not fit in any other category") (figure 7.1).

Figure 7.1
Categories of Humor

Civikly (1986) recommends that teachers who are considering the use of humor review, among other points, how humor has been used in class, that they identify comfortable humor styles, work on "planned spontaneity," and evaluate (with student input) the humor used.

Whether surveying high school students or elementary school students, a "sense of humor" is regularly identified as a characteristic of best-liked teachers and identified as a characteristic lacking among least-liked teachers (Witty 1950). Similar views are held by college students with regard to their professors. Murray's Teacher Behaviors Inventory and Perry's Instructor Expressiveness Construct, found in Wlodkowski's book (1985), among other such communication classification systems, cite "humor" as a key component of enthusiastic teachers. "Humor is also an excellent mnemonic device" (Larson 1982, 198). As a memory aid, humor can help students to visualize a concept, principle, or operation.

Theory, as well as empirical data, points out the close relationship between humor and creativity (Ziv 1989) — an added benefit to the increased use of humor in today's classrooms. Divergent thinking, as defined by Guilford (1959), is enhanced when fear of criticism from one's social environment (classroom) is reduced. "The tension release aspect of laughter and its contagious effects can influence group cohesiveness and thus reduce social anxiety" (Ziv 1989, 114).

Humor can be tendentious — it can help promote a point of view. Johnny Carson's nightly monologue often combined domestic and international political events with humor to make pungent points. We laughed, but we also learned.

We must remember, though, that humor is a tool that should never be used to lower the self-esteem of the student. One must be careful to note the difference between genuine humor, which allows us all to see our more vulnerable human side, and derision, which creates laughter at the expense of another person.

HUMOR: GENDER AND GRADE-LEVEL DIFFERENCES

Are there gender differences in the use of humor by teachers and in student responses to it? Bryant and Zillmann (1988) conclude that, at every level, male teachers were found to use humor more often than female teachers. For instance, Bryant et al. (1980) found that college teachers used an average of 3.34 instances of humor during a fifty-minute class — 3.73 instances for male instructors and 2.43 instances for female instructors. Gorham and Christophel (1990) report a much lower average of only 1.37 humorous attempts by instructors, but still confirm that females' frequency of humor was less (86%) than that of males'.

Humor favoring a particular point, though, is utilized by female professors (62%) to a substantially greater degree than by their male colleagues (43%). Males are more likely to use self-disparaging humor, while females are more likely to have a balance between humor directed at themselves or their students. Self-disparaging humor works best when the speaker and audience are the same sex (Tamborini and Zillmann 1981). Male instructors who used humor generally received higher teaching evaluations, whereas females generally received lower evaluations.

Differences also exist within the audience viewing the humor. Bryant et al. (1980) found that for college students, sexual humor was more appealing to an audience of the opposite sex from that of the teacher. Gorham and Christophel (1990) report that male students are generally more positively affected – indications of learning, attitudes toward course content, and intent to take another course by the same instructor – than female students by teachers' use of humor.

The above citations refer to college instructors who were teaching college-age students, not high school-age adolescents. Neuliep's (1991) study at the high school level reveals that high school teachers' humor differs from their college-level counterparts. High school and mid-high school teachers' self-reports reveal fewer uses of humor. No correlation was found between their years of experience and their frequency of humor use, and no differences were found between award- versus non-award-winning teachers. High school "teachers also indicated that they use humor as a way of putting students at ease, getting students' attention, and for showing that the teacher is human . . . not as a pedagogical strategy for increasing student comprehension or learning" (Neuliep 1991, 354).

CARTOONS: A SAFE FIRST STEP INTO HUMOR

One relatively safe way to begin using humor in the classroom is to incorporate into the curriculum cartoons that carry a message related to the subject being studied. Peterson (1980, 646) reports acquiring, in less than five years, several hundred cartoons with subjects related to his discipline of science. Students' recognition of the point of the cartoon involves a "spontaneous flash of insight that shows a familiar situation in a new light," not unlike the insight that accompanies scientific discoveries. This, he argues, leads to learning.

Neuliep (1991) refers to cartoons as "external source humor" or "third-party" humor. One of the authors, in beginning a discussion of alternatives to punishment, introduces the concept of In-School Suspension, a version of the psychological principle of time-out, by the use of a cartoon. This cartoon, although outrageous and hilarious, uses a mental image and a play

Figure 7.2
In-School Suspension

Drawing courtesy of Mark Fisher.

on words (e.g., in-school suspension versus students physically being suspended in a school) to make its point (figure 7.2). The cartoon, and the chuckles that follow, help reduce student anxiety regarding the upcoming discussion of punishment.

The same author uses another punishment-oriented cartoon depicting two students, both of whom are dusting erasers. One student says to the other, "Hey, wait a minute! You're cleaning erasers as punishment? I'm cleaning erasers as a reward" (*Phi Delta Kappan* 1991, 501). The author's students, in attempting to explain the apparent discrepancy of the cartoon, begin to realize that whether something is a punishment or a reward depends upon the perception of the child receiving it—not the teacher who is handing it out.

Could the same message have been delivered without the cartoon? Sure. But, like a picture, a cartoon is worth a thousand words. Further, cartoons add some welcome variety to a discussion. Lowe (1991) reports that cartoons are especially valuable in large classes where they help maintain student interest, create a visual example of the topic at hand, and add some levity to the class.

Teachers, whether in training or in service, can start a collection of subject-related cartoons for possible inclusion in lectures via overhead transparencies. "It has been demonstrated that some cartoons of suitable type (e.g., visual 'puns') can be used with the intention of serving a direct teaching function such as facilitating the learning of definitions and symbols and promoting insights into difficult concepts" (Powell and Anderson 1985, 87).

Since different subject areas are taught, teachers will likely use different primary sources for amassing a cartoon collection, including professional journals within a specific subject area as well as journals relating to the teaching profession in general. Some wonderful cartoons are included each month in the scholarly journal *Phi Delta Kappan* and the witty *Atlantic Monthly*. At the same time, though, one should not overlook sources such as *Time, Newsweek*, and other magazines, as well as newspapers. Another great source is Brooks' *Best Editorial Cartoons of the Year*, published by Pelican Publishing Company.

Finally, we may want to create our own cartoons. If a teacher does not have the "talent" to do so, he or she could always solicit students who do possess the talent and who, in fact, would be flattered to assist (Demetrulias 1982). One of the authors, on several occasions, has worked with commercial arts students from two local vocational-technical schools who have created original cartoons depicting his subject matter. On more than one occasion, the cartoons have not only been used in class lectures and workshop presentations, but also as pictorials to accompany journal articles published both nationally and internationally.

Before we leave the topic of cartoons, we would like to mention the use of stickers—yes, stickers! Any parent or teacher knows the power over young children that stickers seem to have. Children will do almost anything in the anticipation of receiving "Award" stickers, "Good Job" stickers, or "Thank You" stickers. We believe that there is a use, in moderation, of course, for stickers with older students—even adult students. Is it a little corny? Sure, but so what.

Who doesn't like to be told, whether in words or in symbols (stickers) that they have done a "Good Job" or are deserving of a "Thank You"? In fact, for conveying these messages to teenagers who, because of peer pressure, may be unreceptive to an oral message, stickers are just the trick. Be a little daring. Try peel-away stickers, hip word stickers, and, our favorite, scratch 'n' sniff stickers. Don't overlook the time-honored rubber stamp version of today's sticker craze. "Super," "Nice Work," and "Great Job" stamps or stickers on student work are always appreciated (figure 7.3). Where can you find stickers and motivational rubber stamps? Ask any elementary school teacher. Look in the Yellow Pages for teacher supply stores. By the way, "Thank You" for reading our book.

Figure 7.3
Stickers

BRINGING HUMOR INTO THE CLASSROOM – A GAGGLE OF IDEAS

Although not intended to be a definitive list of suggestions, the following do represent a variety of ways in which humor can be brought into the classroom. Of course, humor *never* is used at a student's expense.

- Use a humorous cartoon to introduce a lesson. Encourage students to locate and then bring in their own subject-related cartoons, puns, and so on.
- Share a humorous event from your life in the form of [Ha, Ha] "a funny thing happened to me on the way to the Forum." Solicit such events from your students' lives.
- When a story or pun flops, try holding up your grade book and repeating the pun that has just flopped. Then there will be laughter.
- When citing a string of examples of a concept, end with a humorous or unexpected event. When teaching the classroom management concept of "time-out," for instance, one could offer examples such as the child being made to sit in a corner, standing out in the hall, or spending a day with your accountant! When teaching the concept of "positive reinforcement," one could offer examples such as scratch-and-sniff stickers, consumables (e.g., candy), or a shiny, red Maserati!
- Include appropriate humor on tests. In a multiple-choice question, have one of the "a" though "e" choices be some outrageous distractor. Every once in a while, toss in Elvis, Kermit-the-Frog, or perhaps even your name.
- Encourage students to incorporate humor in answering test questions. Divergent thinking – creativity – will be enhanced.
- Bury, perhaps in a cigar box, humor that dies – and some of it will. Conduct a brief "grave-site" ceremony, and move on (Herbert 1991). If you are so inclined, you could slip into a short dance routine as Johnny Carson did when his monologue died.
- Start a humor board where everyone can put up their favorite cartoons, subject-related or not (your choice), with an award for the best one each week.
- Look for the humorous side of situations that probably are going to occur anyhow. Something that falls to the floor could elicit a "Gravity is proven once again" comment, or a truck backing up outside with a loud "beep, beep, beep" sound could evoke an "Ok, whose wristwatch alarm is that?" statement from the instructor.
- Combine humor with other acting/teaching skills (e.g., use of props) such as donning a pair of "Wellees" (Wellington boots) while telling students that, "We are going to do some 'deep' thinking today." Keep those boots handy for the times when students try to bluff their way through an answer. Bring out the boots, hold them up high, and say, "Boy, it's getting kind of 'deep' in here." In the future, simply holding up the boots will make your point and engender laughter.

- Have students write "humorous" lyrics to seasonal songs, perhaps Christmas carols as does Patricia Thomas, a physics teacher from Northeast High School in Pinellas County, Florida. Join the students in traveling the halls singing the "carols." An example of such a "carol" would be:

"Gravity" (sung to the tune of "Jingle Bells")

> A comet hits the earth.
> It's made of methane gas.
> It makes a giant force.
> Now isn't that so nice.
>
> Gravity, Gravity,
> keeps us on the ground.
> An apple fell on Newton,
> he said, what goes up comes down.
>
> Gravity, Gravity,
> mass times nine-point eight.
> Remember, travel very fast,
> if earth you must escape.

Everyone finds the experience humorous, but like all of the acting skills highlighted in this book, the humor has an academic purpose.

- Comment upon one's own hand-drawn overhead transparencies or chalkboard sketches with the statement, "It is pretty obvious why I didn't major in art."
- As a teacher of grammar—aren't all teachers?—show students Victor Borge's classic act in which he reads a piece of literature and, using sound effects, highlights the punctuation. Grammar will never again be seen as dull.
- Keep a skeleton (miniature will do) in the classroom closet—give it a name. Bring it out occasionally and "include" him/her in the class discussions. One could substitute a life-size picture of Joe Paterno or Albert Einstein for the skeleton. Even a Chia Pet would do.
- When stumbling over one's words in a lecture (especially likely to happen early on a Monday morning), comment, "Gosh, I forgot to put my upper plate of dentures in this morning."

SUMMARY

According to Cornett (1986), humor can be a powerful instructional resource that helps teachers in a number of ways including attracting attention, improving communication, soothing difficult moments, and reinforcing desired behaviors. The appropriate use of humor is a powerful tool that can help educators positively affect changes in a student's knowledge, attitudes, skills, and aspirations (Warnock 1989).

Having highlighted the power of using humor in the classroom, it seems appropriate to offer some general cautions. While the intuitive benefits of humor may now seem obvious, there are recent research studies (MacAdam 1985, 329) that conclude that instructors who use humor may "contradict student expectations of just how a college teacher is 'supposed' to act."

Sophisticated and subtle humor may be one of the hardest kinds of communication to understand and appreciate. It may demand a level of knowledge and intelligence that may not exist in some classrooms (Armour 1975). Not all students may catch the "point" in a pun. If it has to be explained, unintended embarrassment may replace the intended humor.

Another caution regarding humor applies to novice teachers. According to Wandersee (1982), beginning teachers may well decide to postpone using humor until they begin to feel confident in discipline, organization, and content mastery. Humor usage entails some risk on the part of the teacher. Too many risks too early in a teacher's career could backfire.

Recognizing the cautions described above, it still is generally felt that humor holds the potential for helping teachers to teach more effectively. Humor can also help the teacher him/herself. Humor, and the laughter it precipitates, may have medicinal value. According to Walter (1990), each time you chuckle or "crack up," your brain releases natural painkilling hormones which, in turn, trigger the release of endorphins, natural opiates that can reduce pain, make eyes sparkle, and get the brain to work more effectively. He also claims that laughter can increase your feelings of self-esteem and may help you lose weight!

Humor, Humphreys (1990) argues, has positive effects on one's immune functions, pain, circulation and respiration, and physical illness. The medical and physiological impact of humor, often described as "gut" laughing or "stationary jogging," is well researched and well supported. Neilsen (1993), for instance, cites over one-hundred references in support of humor's body- and mind-curing powers. In a stressful field such as teaching, curing powers can be helpful!

"One of the greatest sins in teaching is to be boring. It's a dull moment when there is no whetstone for the wit. Work mixed with fun goes better," says Baughman (1979, 28). Humor, according to Woods (1983, 112), "facilitates the task of teaching and learning and obviates strain." When students and teachers laugh together, they stop for a time being separated by individuality, authority, and age. They become a unit; they enjoy a shared experience. If that sense of community can be sustained and applied to the job of thinking, a more positive learning environment will have been created (Highet 1950; MacAdam 1985). We agree.

Properly used, humor clearly sends the message that you are confident, comfortable, *and* in control. The fear of feeling foolish when attempting humor should be, in part, offset by the aphorism, "Education should teach us to play the wise fool rather than the solemn ass" (Herbert 1991, 17). While not all teachers can or should act like a Johnny Carson or David Letterman at the chalkboard, the thoughtful, spontaneous, or planned use of instructional humor can bring the wonder of play, wit, and wisdom (Korobkin 1988) into a classroom. Humor contributes positively to our perceived identity in the role of teacher—the "teacher-self." Clearly, humor is a skill that should be developed by all teachers.

THROUGH THE STUDENTS' EYES

When surveyed regarding the use of humor in the classroom, students offered real-life examples such as those that follow. Although each example refers to the use of humor in a particular subject area, the application to other disciplines is evident.

Like, Like . . .

Mr. C. will forever be my favorite teacher because he was entertaining. In order to break the monotony of learning geometry definitions, whenever any student tried to define a term and used the word "like," that student would have to stop immediately and walk a lap around the classroom. Once he had completed this humorous act, he would sit down and then redefine the geometry term. This quickly led students to learn their definitions, and, if they could not repeat them verbatim, they could at least describe them in plain and clear English. Trust me, not too many students in the class said "like" for any reason after the first two weeks.

Sick Herbie

My math teacher loaned his shiny metal chalkholder, named "Herbie," to students when he asked them to do math problems on the front board. He told the students that Herbie rarely made a mistake. Any mistakes, if made, had to be due to a "sick Herbie." If he (Herbie) made a mistake, he would excuse himself to go to the trash can. Herbie then would return all cured—sporting a beautiful, long, white piece of chalk.

THE MASTER'S VOICE

For further discussion of the concepts and skills presented in this chapter, read the following paragraphs in Appendix II: Testimonials from Award-Winning College Professors: Clough, 5; Lavin and Lewis, 9–11, 18, 23; Lisska, 1; Mahoney, 3; Rotkin, 1, 2.

CHAPTER 8

ROLE-PLAYING

To be confident, act confident.
— Eison

INTRODUCTION

Role-playing means temporarily transforming oneself into a different person by means of modifications of expression and appearance, or by the use of props and language. To play a role successfully, one must become someone else and do so convincingly, at least for the moment. Obviously, it is a process that is totally synonymous with the profession of acting. In addition, it can be a very valuable tool for the classroom teacher.

Let us clarify at the start that our intention here is to address the means by which the teacher, *not the students*, can engage in role-playing. Considerable work has been done on the pedagogical value of student role-playing, and that is treated extensively in other texts. The rationale by which we decide to use student role-playing to intensify the learning experience, however, also applies to the use of *teacher* role-playing. Consequently, the teacher as actor is worthy of our consideration.

Actors, like teachers, are involved in role-playing at two different levels. The second, more obvious level is their involvement in the character of the play, but the first level is their involvement in the "role" of actor per se. The *person* James Earl Jones or Jessica Tandy is slightly different from the *actor* James Earl Jones or Jessica Tandy because the person must assume the role of a more confident and public self in order to succeed as an actor. Many actors are reported to have observed that they can feel a transformation of self occurring each time they don their makeup or costume or walk on stage. The transformation is not just into the character being portrayed but, more fundamentally, into the role of "actor." Since both levels of role-playing are appropriate for the teacher as well, both will be addressed in this chapter.

CREATION OF YOUR PROFESSIONAL PERSONA

Earlier in this book, we have referred to Hanning's observations (1984) concerning the challenges of the beginning teacher. His comments are particularly apropos here: he suggests that the beginner can make him/herself a better teacher by the process of "role mastery."

Teachers would benefit from that advice, regardless of career level. That is, consider the attributes, behaviors, and appearance that come to mind when you think of the role of "teacher." Each of us probably envisions some slightly different combination of features. Perhaps you see a straightbacked person walking with authority and pride; another may see a kindly, parental figure hovering about students with interest and concern. Whatever the visual image, it can serve as the basis for the creation of your own role — your "teacher-self."

The studies of Kress and Ehrlichs (1990), Butler et al. (1980), and Ostrand and Creaser (1978) all confirm that there are positive correlations between role-playing the part of a person whom one aspires to be and the development of one's self-esteem. While these studies did not include the teaching profession, nonetheless their conclusions seem applicable. By *acting* like the professional you want to be, your self-confidence will likely improve, thus allowing you to *be* that professional. That hypothesis is confirmed in the experiences of many successful teachers who note that they are less shy and more dynamic when putting on their "teacher role" (Hanning 1984).

As with role-play in general, playing the teacher role may require some costuming in order to be most successful. In this case, of course, we are not speaking of theatrical costumes, but rather minor elements of attire that may make us *feel* more like that professional we aspire to represent. You may feel more like a teacher by carrying a briefcase, for instance, or wearing a lapel membership pin, high heels, or a particular necktie. There is no single "uniform" for the role of teacher. If a particular outfit or accessory makes you feel more confident in your teacher role, then wear it. It's that simple.

An example from a related professional area seems appropriate to include here because it is so telling of the value of costuming. The case in point was the experience of a member of the clergy queried about why she chose to wear the heavy ministerial robes on the hottest Sunday of the year. Her reply was that by wearing the "costume" of the clergy, she felt more confident in the role of pastor and thus was more likely to be received attentively and respectfully by persons unaccustomed to a woman minister. Her self-confidence, she felt, would have a positive impact on her communication success. Her experience is absolutely consistent with all that we know about self-confidence and communication and certainly testifies to the value of a little costuming for role-playing to create a persona.

While some degree of a professional "costume" may be helpful in creating the role of teacher, it is not a prerequisite. The most important precondition for successful role creation is simply to have identified the characteristics of the teacher you aspire to possess. Then, using some combination of expression, posture, appearance, and language, act that role in your classroom. In doing so, remember that the goal of this teacher role-playing is the enhancement of self-confidence. One should not act the role to become manipulative.

CREATION OF A CHARACTER

In addition to playing the role of teacher, we can play an innumerable assortment of character roles in order to enliven our classroom instruction. While acting the role of teacher will boost our self-confidence, acting the other roles may require a greater proportion of courage. Because role-playing is such a vivid and enriching instructional tool, however, it merits the effort. Interestingly, one veteran teacher/role-player was moved initially to attempt some role-playing as a remedy for his shyness (Barto 1986). An English teacher and Thoreau scholar, Barto was struggling with the challenge of stimulating students when he remembered the advice of Thoreau himself: we should not be afraid to do things that others may consider "different" when our instinct tells us that "different" may be better. In this case, being different meant being Thoreau for a time. Let us take a closer look at the whys and wherefores of creating a character for our classes.

GOALS AND VALUES

One of the more memorable examples of educational role-playing occurred in a radio series some years ago called "Meeting of the Minds." The program, produced and moderated by Steve Allen, consisted of hypothetical conversations among great intellects of the past discussing contemporary issues. Allen, of course, played all the roles, from Aristotle to Zoroaster and everyone in between. The important point here is why Allen chose the role-playing vehicle for this program. His goal was an educational one: he wanted the contemporary public to appreciate the sage insights from the past and be stimulated to discuss the issues themselves. One could have attempted to accomplish that goal via a more conventional lecture-discussion approach. But, in Allen's view, that approach would not hold the listeners' attention nor be very provocative; something more dramatic was needed. We would concur.

Role-playing enlivens material. By portraying a character pertinent to the specific subject matter, the teacher is able to make abstract concepts more concrete, to hold the students' attention, to clarify depths of meaning, and to stimulate student reflection on the material covered.

Numerous teachers who have tried playing a role confirm the success of the tool in motivating their students and provoking them to a more thorough understanding of the material. For instance, a political science professor in Idaho observed that his students answered test questions about characters he had portrayed in his occasional role-plays more accurately than questions about figures who had been discussed more traditionally in class (Duncombe and Heikkinen 1988). Others from disciplines as disparate as history, English, foreign language, and physical science all report that their goal was to motivate students ("Not so Rich" 1993; Carroll 1991; "Our Readers" 1982).

The current generation of high school and college students is definitely visually oriented. This has been attested to and decried in numerous arenas. Those teachers who engage in occasional role-playing are simply adjusting to that reality about their students instead of bewailing it. The students are more attentive and will learn better when presented with the material in a visually stimulating manner. Teacher role-plays accomplish this goal.

Not only is role-playing a motivating device for students, it is also a freeing device. By pretending to be someone else for a while, the teacher has created a situation in which students seem to feel freer to challenge and question ideas presented (Duncombe and Heikkinen 1988). After all, that person up front is not the grade-dispensing class mentor, but rather a member of Washington's army or a Puritan woman, for example. In one study in which the teachers role-played the part of their students, the observers noted that the students seemed to feel freer to discuss their problems than before the teachers acted out certain situations (Barcinas and Gozer 1986).

The goals, then, of teacher role-play are multifaceted. The strategy may be used to motivate students, to hold their attention, to clarify or intensify material, and/or to stimulate discussion. If any of these needs exist in our classrooms, the portrayal of a relevant character is a possible teaching tool to be considered.

Before going on to describe the specific elements involved in doing role-play, it should be emphasized that this is a tool that can accomplish those pedagogical goals only if used in moderation. If the students become too accustomed to the teacher being someone else, the role-play has lost the element of surprise and has been diminished in interest value. To work, role-play should essentially be a tool kept in the "bottom of the tool box" to be used somewhat rarely for special emphasis and impact.

THE PROCESS

Everyone who has performed a classroom characterization agrees on one key point: it *must* be well prepared. While we may use student role-plays on a somewhat spontaneous basis, teacher role-play will be only as valuable as the advance planning that has gone into it. That is where the process of role-playing begins.

Specifically, the teacher must begin by carefully choosing and researching an appropriate character to portray. It could be an obvious choice — the central figure in the material being studied, or it could be something more creative. The art teacher speaking *as* Andrew Wyeth is able to convey one perspective; speaking as Wyeth's model, on the other hand, would enable the development of a very different perspective. The character simply must be one that you, the teacher, are comfortable with (Barto 1986).

Research about the character should focus on biographical data as well as information about the times and setting in which this character lived. Sufficient information must be gathered to allow you to develop a sense, not just of the person's actions, ideas, and achievements, but also of his/her feelings, values, and attitudes.

In doing so, the teacher is ready for the second step in the process of character creation — deciding about costuming and props. By studying the character thoroughly, you will develop a sense of how this person would have dressed, stood, moved, and behaved. Knowing that, you must determine the degree to which you wish to recreate the person visually — a total costume may not always be necessary, appropriate, or comfortable. It is a matter of personal choice whether to *imitate* the character (full costume, props, and staging) or *suggest* the character (minimal costume and props, no staging). Some amount of props will generally make the role-player feel the part more fully and will assist in creating a more credible representation for the students.

Third, the dialogue must be constructed. In choosing what words to say, decisions should once again grow out of the research done on the character. Inasmuch as possible, using the person's exact words would be appropriate. That makes the characterization valid and conveys more clearly that the speaker is *not* Professor X, but a completely different character. When verbatim texts of the person's speech cannot be found or are not suitable, a script should be prepared using a manner of speech that seems consistent with the person's character and intellect. The more comfortable you feel with the character, the more you may want to build into the script some openings for spontaneous dialogue with the students. Be prepared to remain in character, no matter how the students respond.

Once the materials for the role-play are assembled and rehearsed, it is time for the final step in the process, the actual performance. There is no one right way to initiate the role-play in class. In some cases, it may be fitting to prepare the students in advance for the arrival of this character, having them do some research and prepare questions. In other cases, the teacher may simply appear in character unheralded and begin to speak. Both approaches have advantages and disadvantages which would need to be evaluated relevant to the particular class for which the role-play is intended.

No matter how the role-play is initiated, it is critical that it be brought effectively to a close. There should be an opportunity for "debriefing" either at the end of the class period or on the succeeding day to monitor the impressions the students actually had about the "guest." This is necessary because role-playing is such a dramatic device that it is possible some students may have gotten caught up in one of the characterization's special elements and missed the overall point. Naturally, a well-prepared and well-executed role-play will diminish the chances of such error. Check to be sure.

The teacher's creation of a character is a process moving from selection, research, planning, costuming, scripting, and rehearsing to presentation and review. If that sounds like the same process that an actor goes through in creating a character, it is not coincidental!

APPLICATIONS

The circumstances in which a character portrayal may be a suitable teaching vehicle are as numerous and far-ranging as the subject matter taught. A few specific examples may help you visualize the possibilities.

At the high school level, two noteworthy examples would be those provided by American history teacher Spencer Johnson ("Not so Rich" 1993) and English teacher David Barto (Barto 1986). Johnson portrays famous and "less than famous" citizens of eighteenth- and nineteenth-century America ranging from a Plains Indian to a member of Washington's army. His portrayals, done in authentic costumes, have earned him such a following that he is now a regular part of reenactment programs in the summer. Similarly, Barto's portrayals of Henry David Thoreau have earned him such acclaim that he has been asked to do various one-man shows at conventions and commemorative celebrations. He tends to use a little less elaborate costuming, but always tries to incorporate props appropriate to the character and times to help set the mood for his students.

It should be emphasized that neither Johnson nor Barto came into the teaching profession as actors. Rather, they "fell into" the role-playing technique out of the desperation of trying to find some way to motivate their students. In both cases, it worked so well that it is now a standard part of their teaching.

Photo 8.1
Tycho Brahe

Photo courtesy of Dennis Murray.

Similarly, a junior high science teacher in Pennsylvania, Dennis Murray, was looking for some vehicle by which he could excite his students at least a little about science (Carroll 1991). His reflections resulted in a decision to use the character of Tycho Brahe (sixteenth-century Danish astronomer) to "speak" to the students about the principles of physical science (photo 8.1). It has turned out to have been a very wise decision. His full-costumed Brahe, speaking with the arrogance for which he was known, has stimulated students in a way no standard lecture could have done. In his case, the dramatization even includes background music and staging, in addition to the custom-made costume.

A less elaborate, but equally successful example of teacher role-play is the "two-hat" technique used by political science professor Stanley Duncombe (Duncombe and Heikkinen 1988). The gist of the technique is a staged debate between real or hypothetical persons representing opposing political viewpoints. Duncombe plays both characters and distinguishes the speakers simply by putting on a hat appropriate to the different characters and positions. While the costuming is minimal, the characterizations are no less valid, since they grow out of considerable research.

One of the authors has used a version of this "two-hat" technique in the form of a t-shirt that he dons when staging a hypothetical debate between B. F. Skinner, a behaviorist, and Carl Rogers, a humanist, and the opposing philosophies they represent. The t-shirt, prepared at one of those shopping mall kiosks that place pictures on almost anything (calendars, coffee mugs, hats, t-shirts), has pictures of Skinner and Rogers facing each other as if in heated debate. This same author also uses Duncombe's "two-hat" technique in the form of a collection of baseball-type caps, each of which is adorned with pictures of famous men and women representing his subject area.

While the stagecraft of the above examples varies considerably, the quality of preparation is the same. After much work, the teachers have chosen to recreate a character whose presence in the classroom has been a riveting presentation enhancing the impact and meaningfulness of the subject matter.

STORYTELLING

A variation on role-play involving significantly less staging but having similar effects is storytelling. A much simpler and briefer technique than the role-playing we have described, it is still a form of role-play in that the teacher takes on a different persona, the role of narrator. The art of the storyteller is a time-honored tradition in many cultures and has carried over very effectively to the classroom. No matter the age of the students, there is still a noticeably captivating effect when one says "once upon a time" or something equivalent.

One of the most legendary of classroom storytellers points out the educational power of a story to hold students' attention, teach values, and nurture the imagination (Shedlock 1951). That perspective was confirmed by more recent research on the value of narratives. This research concluded that the opening of a story signals to students that literal meaning is being highlighted or emphasized (Nussbaum, Comadena, and Holladay 1987). Thus the storytelling episode stimulates and refocuses their attention.

Whether the story told be truth or fiction, it is told best if told simply. The teacher should play the part of narrator as well as any and all other characters in the story using slight modifications of posture or expression to suggest the identity of the character speaking. As with the more extensive role-plays, storytelling may incorporate some dialogue with the students. However, since storytelling should usually consume no more that ten or fifteen minutes, inviting student dialogue may result in an inappropriate and misleading digression that detracts from the story's point.

SUMMARY

Teacher role-playing is the pedagogical tool probably most resembling the tools of the actor. Consequently, it may be the most difficult for many teachers. If a teacher's self-confidence is still "under construction," the one role-play that is ideal is the role of teacher itself. We benefit by acting in the way that we think confident, successful teachers act because we actually grow into the role, *becoming* confident master teachers ourselves. Once that self-esteem begins to develop, we may want to try the creation of character roles to further enhance our teaching. All role-playing should be carefully planned, rehearsed, and presented in a well-organized manner. By doing so, you will have added another enlivening tool to your repertoire.

THROUGH THE STUDENTS' EYES

When surveyed regarding the use of role-playing in the classroom, students offered real-life examples such as those that follow. Although each example refers to the use of role-playing in a particular subject area, the application to other disciplines is evident.

Storytelling

My sociology teacher is very effective because he makes an effort to show that he truly cares about his students and their grasp of the subject matter, which is difficult in a class of eight-hundred students. He does this, in part, by telling stories that we can relate to in an entertaining manner that holds our attention. It's much easier to learn in this positive, friendly environment.

My Friend George

My eleventh grade history teacher was very enthusiastic about his subject. When explaining something, he would act as if he knew George Washington, or whoever it was he was talking about. He would laugh about something that person had said or done just as if he were there while it was happening. He didn't just teach history as if it were a collection of facts; he taught it as if it were a story about someone he knew.

High Official

My teacher stood up on his desk (space utilization) and, with a silly smirk on his face, looked around the classroom as if he were superior to us. On his shirt he wore a paper sign that said, "F for fluorine." Then he exclaimed, "I am the highest official on this planet called electro-negativity!" On the desks were copies of the periodic chart. Then it hit me — we, the students, were elements on the periodic chart — all with lower electro-negativities than fluorine.

The Russians Are Coming

My tenth-grade teacher showed up for class dressed in a long, red Russian robe which prominently displayed a hammer and sickle and a small star above them. He told us that the robe stood for revolution; the hammer and sickle represented united workers; and the star stood for the Communist Party. He began the history lesson by speaking a little bit of Russian. He then played the Russian anthem for the class, while at the same time demonstrating a short Russian dance by folding his arms in front of him and moving his legs about. I don't know about the rest of the class, but the costume and dance left a visual impression with me and helped bring the lesson into focus.

My Dear Aunt Sally

My algebra teacher, Mrs. U, dressed up as a wretched old woman named Aunt Sally. She then began her lesson on the correct order of mathematical functions: powers (Pity), parentheses (Pity), multiply (My), divide (Dear), add (Aunt), and subtract (Sally). All I had to do was think of Aunt Sally and her gnarled cane in order to remember the order of mathematical operations.

THE MASTER'S VOICE

For further discussion of the concepts and skills presented in this chapter, read the following paragraphs in Appendix II: Testimonials from Award-Winning College Professors: Harrison, 3, 4, 10; Lavin and Lewis, 12–15; Light, 3; Mahoney, 4, 5; McBrayer, 1, 3; Richardson, 2, 3.

CHAPTER 9

PROPS

Give me a lever long enough
And a prop strong enough,
I can single handed move the world.
—Archimedes

INTRODUCTION

Perhaps Archimedes placed a bit too much confidence in his "prop." This prop, though, is central to the success of his goal of moving the world. Classroom teachers may not be asked to move the world, but they are asked to motivate students — at times a task of seemingly equal proportion! It has been argued that many school programs err on the side of too much book work and too little hands-on work (Sukow 1990) — the latter often relies upon the use of props.

Although actor Hal Holbrook may be able to stand on a prop-less stage and command the attention of an audience as he portrays Mark Twain, most stage and film productions rely heavily on the use of props. In fact, awards are given for such props, for example, costumes. Even Holbrook uses costume props. In order better to depict the role of Twain, Holbrook dresses the part of a Southern gentleman complete with his white hair, white suit, broad-brimmed hat, and cigar.

If a picture (a two-dimensional image) is worth a thousand words, then a prop (a three-dimensional image) must be worth much more. Props help set the stage. They convey information which is often crucial to the film's or play's message. Period-specific props, such as colorful homes on Long Island, ladies in shimmering dresses, and expensive cars, paint the picture of the Roaring Twenties — those carefree, affluent, no feeling-of-responsibility days of F. Scott Fitzgerald's *The Great Gatsby*. Still other props, such as tent cities, barefoot children, dusty roads, and possession-filled vehicles paint a picture of the desperation and hopelessness of the people in the film version of John Steinbeck's *The Grapes of Wrath*.

PROPS UNIQUE TO SPECIFIC SUBJECT MATTER

Although some subject areas may come more immediately to mind in their reliance upon props (e.g., biology, anthropology), no area is exempt from the benefits of using props. The use of props in each discipline holds the potential for securing students' attention and providing information. Even the simplest of props, such as those effectively used in the almost MTV-style Disney Production, *Bill Nye: The Science Guy,* can do the trick. Bill Nye makes subjects such as "sound" and "motion" come alive using everyday props common in most homes or schools.

This is an everyday occurrence in many different subject areas. For example, what anthropologist would not rely heavily upon animal and plant fossils, whether in the form of pictures, plastic replicas, or, when possible, the real thing? Would a geography teacher attempt to teach geography without turning students' attention to maps? Would a geometry teacher consider teaching without his or her compass and protractor? Who could envision a history professor teaching the American Civil War without period-specific artifacts and relics? What literature teacher would teach Shakespeare without first decorating the room with theater posters of *Richard III, Hamlet, Julius Caesar,* or *Macbeth* in order to create the proper mood?

What biology instructor would not have collections of things suspended in formaldehyde or could resist leaf collection assignments? What chemistry professor would teach the principles of chemistry without relying upon bunsen burners, pipettes, graduated cylinders, test tubes, and litmus paper? Could a physics teacher teach mechanical advantage without demonstrating the concept with levers, inclined planes, and stationary and movable pulleys?

Speaking of physics teachers, we know of one, Jonathan Hall, who demonstrates the concepts of force and pressure by having an eager undergraduate student nail two pieces of wood together—on the teacher's chest (photo 9.1). In an experiment, not all that different from the Indian guru who astonishes followers by "sleeping" on a bed of nails, Professor Hall dramatically makes his point.

Even a subject such as accounting, that doesn't seem to lend itself to the use of props, can with a little creativity use props as teaching aids. A professor friend of ours describes how such household props as a picnic basket, kitchen measuring devices, a stocked linen closet, and a wastebasket can be used to teach the accounting concepts of a "T" account, the liability/capital equation, inventory pricing, and the closing entry, respectively.

Photo 9.1
"Nailing" a Teacher

PROPS GENERIC TO ALL SUBJECT MATTER

Some props, such as the physics professor's bed of nails, are subject specific; others are more universal in nature. Take, for example, an apple. In an art class, the apple may be used as a still-life prop to be painted. In a chemistry class, the apple may be used to test the reaction of oxygen with the apple once it has been peeled. The significance of taking a bite out of the forbidden apple may be explored in a religion class. The historical accuracy of Newton's having been hit on the head with a falling apple could be investigated. And, as shown in the film *Stand and Deliver*, Jamie Escalante, the Bolivian-born Los Angeles calculus teacher, could use an apple and a knife to teach fundamental concepts in mathematics.

Another example of a generic prop is the telephone. One education professor we know carries a portable phone to class early in the semester waiting for the inevitable student who will come in late. When the student enters, the professor, pretending the phone has rung, answers it and acts out a dialogue as if it were a parent calling to inquire why her child's teacher was not in the classroom when he was supposed to have been. Her child was bullied by several other children, and the teacher was not there to intervene. The words "attorney," "negligence," and "sue" enter the conversation. The phone is then handed to the student, and he or she is asked to explain the absence to the irate parent. This use of a prop, along with a little role-playing (another acting skill), is an effective lesson for the teacher-training student — one that will be remembered, hopefully, for life.

As a prop, a phone could be used for other "pretend" calls — perhaps to "the President" in a government class, to NASA astronauts in a science class, to Apple Computer in a marketing class, or to Socrates in a philosophy class (very long distance!). The possibilities are endless. One could, of course, use the phone to make actual calls. The phone could be a real prop linking the classroom with real people from the community and from across the world.

What about using a piece of taffy (candy) as a prop? One college professor we know takes several pieces of salt-water taffy with him to class. At an appropriate point in the lecture, he stops talking, takes out a piece of taffy, unwraps it, chews it, and slowly "digests" it — a bodily function that he would like his students to emulate mentally with the subject matter he has just presented. After the food-for-thought has been digested, he entertains student questions and/or comments. There never fails to be a student response. He attributes it all to his taffy prop.

Lowman (1984) suggests that even an everywhere-present, taken-for-granted book can be an effective generic prop. As an example, he cites the positive effect of a teacher reading a quote directly from a book rather than from his or her notes. The words may be the same, but the dramatic impact is different. Reading from a book adds a dimension of reality; reading from one's notes is a step further removed from reality. Lowman points out that the prop does not have to communicate anything directly; it is not even critical that students can see it closely. Props, books or otherwise, are used for visual variety and to refresh student attention.

PROPS AND TECHNOLOGY

Although this section, too, applies to the generic usefulness of props, it has been separated from the one above because here the medium of communication itself becomes the prop. Such universal props include handouts, flip charts, chalkboards, overhead projectors (transparencies), films, computers, and other electronic media. An informative handout is as valuable for an English class as for a sociology class. A flip chart, sometimes with prepared pages, is as useful for a psychology class as for a speech class. The humble chalkboard (sometimes in the version of today's felt marker board) also continues as a mainstay classroom prop in every subject area.

Besides being informative, a prop, properly used, can be a form of security blanket for the teacher. For instance, outlining the major points of one's lesson on an overhead transparency before class has several advantages. By having a student seated near the projector uncover, upon command, designated portions of the overhead, the instructor is free to move about the room taking advantage of another acting skill, space utilization. Further, revealing just a little of the transparency at a time ("strip-tease" method) can add suspense—still another acting skill.

PRESENTING A PROP

Whether the prop is subject specific or not, whether it is purchased or instructor-prepared, or whether it is low or high tech, it must be presented. *How* it is presented or used can make or break the success of the lesson. A rule of thumb central to any effective use of props is that one should practice with the prop before going on stage (using it in the classroom). For instance, all movies, filmstrips, and other audiovisual media should be previewed. Not to do so is, at best, to waste time and, at worst, to invite disaster. Overhead transparencies should be "tested" to see if they are clear and large enough to be seen from any corner of the room. For any and all projector-type devices, check to see if there is a spare projector bulb, if an extension cord is required, and if the room can be sufficiently darkened. Is the film already threaded? If not, do you know how to thread it?

"Dry runs" of all experiments, whether in science or psychology, should be done. Do you know how to take apart and reassemble a recently purchased model, for example, the human brain for psychology? Is there chalk available for the chalkboard? Are the felt markers serviceable, or have they run dry? Are there any erasers? Do you have masking tape handy to use when hanging posters or student work? Would thumb tacks work better?

Ponder the advantages and disadvantages of passing the prop around the class for closer scrutiny. If a teacher has only one prop to pass around, students fall into three categories: those that have already viewed it, those who are viewing it, and those who have not viewed it. Even if there is a prop for everyone, weigh the benefits versus the drawbacks of passing them out. Do you have the time to pass them out and collect them again? Will students be attending to different parts of the prop than that upon which you want them to focus?

Consider varying your strategy, from keeping the prop hidden from students' view until it is ready to be used, to placing it in a conspicuous place well ahead of the time you plan to use it. The former may heighten student surprise; the latter may heighten student suspense.

Keep props simple. "Remember that a visual aid should be exactly that — an aid, not the complete source of information" (Bradley 1981, 267). Avoid talking to the prop, unless, of course, that is the purpose of using the prop, as would be the case with a puppet or pretend phone call.

USING STUDENTS AS PROPS

One special set of props are the students themselves. Everyone, though not necessarily volunteering to do so, loves to be "on stage." Several examples of how to use students as props follow.

Displacement Theory

One instructor that we know teaches the "displacement theory" in chemistry by assigning three students to play the role of elements. While one girl is assigned the role of chlorine (Cl), two boys, respectively, are assigned the roles of sodium (Na) and potassium (K). The students are called to the front of the room and 3-M Post-Its with the designated Na, K, or Cl symbols are placed on each student's chest.

Na and Cl are now told to hold hands, forming NaCl (sodium chloride), and are instructed to walk slowly across the room. K has eyes for Cl. Since K is the more active element, he wrestles with and displaces Na. The net result is KCl holding hands and Na, the less active element, left all alone — displaced. Corny? Perhaps. Remembered? Yes.

Figure 9.1
Glass of Floating Ice

Drawing courtesy of Mark Fisher.

Why Does Ice Float?

Another professor in physics tackles the mystery of "Why does ice float?" through the use of student props. At first, students show no sense of amazement at the fact that ice floats (figure 9.2). They just take it for granted that this is how the world operates. If ice didn't float, most northerly bodies of fresh water would freeze solid during the winter, melting only slightly during the summer months. Ice is the only solid that when dropped into its own liquid form, floats! Why? (Note that we have slipped in a little suspense!)

In order to demonstrate what happens, nine student volunteers are called to the front of the room, each assigned to play the role of a water molecule. The students form three rows of three, standing about two feet apart. The instructor pretends to turn down the temperature in the room and asks the student molecules what their natural response would be. Most respond by moving a little closer together, thus becoming more dense – heavier. When the temperature is "turned down" some more, the molecules respond by getting still closer together, thus still more dense – heavier.

The trend is clear, the colder the water, the more dense (heavier) the water. If we lower the temperature enough for water to turn to ice, the trend should continue. Ice should be heavier than its surrounding water and thus stay submerged. Students are surprised to find out that from 4 degrees centigrade down to 0 degrees centigrade, water molecules actually move further apart, becoming less dense (less heavy) than the surrounding water. Thus ice floats; it doesn't sink! The student "molecules," as well as the audience observing these live props, will never forget this lesson.

Discrimination

Finally, who doesn't recognize the impression-forming activity used to teach the feelings of inferiority experienced when one is discriminated against? An example of such an activity would be that "all blond-haired students" must enter the school from the school's rear doors, only use designated drinking fountains, and sit at the back of the classroom. Reading about discrimination is one thing; experiencing it firsthand is another.

SUMMARY

Do you remember "show and tell" days of kindergarten years? The prop, the "show," was used as sort of a crutch to promote the real reason for the exercise, the "tell." And it worked! The teller's words were more informative through the use of the prop. "Show and tell" works for all ages. The use of physical teaching props, as good educational practice, cuts across various educational settings (Mark 1989).

From the flowing gowns and bubbles of "The Lawrence Welk Show" to the fast pace of MTV, from a Royal Shakespearian production of *Richard III* to a second grade holiday pageant, and from teaching biology to teaching literature, props are a key ingredient in helping to set the stage and in conveying the intended message.

In addition to the potential for "pizzazz" that the use of props provides, they also can provide a sense of security for the teacher. Whether used as part of a demonstration or held up as an example, a good prop can help clarify a difficult idea as well as enliven an otherwise less-than-stimulating concept.

At times the use of a prop may demand improvisation on the part of a teacher. As any actor will tell you, improvisation can be challenging. Since most props do not come complete with a set of directions, teachers must use their imagination and creativity. Take the lowly apple. Is it just a fruit to eat, or could it be a prop? Could we paint it in art class? Could we divide it in mathematics class? Could we discuss that the Japanese are reluctant to import it? Could we spell it? Could we examine the effect exposure to the air has on it once the skin has been broken? Could we eat it, one bite at a time, as a way to show that most tasks, no matter how difficult, are best mastered one step at a time? Improvise — the possibilities are limitless.

THROUGH THE STUDENTS' EYES

When surveyed regarding the use of props in the classroom, students offered real-life examples such as those that follow. Although each example refers to the use of props in a particular subject area, the application to other disciplines is evident.

38th Parallel

Mr. B., my high school history teacher, made the study of World War II and the Korean Conflict more interesting because he had experienced both firsthand. While talking about his personal experiences, he showed us some of the weapons, clothing, and equipment used during these conflicts. I learned more in this class than in any other dealing with American wars.

Roy G. Biv

Mrs. T. brought in a very large doll that, literally, was dressed in every color of the rainbow.   This prop, introduced as Mr. Roy G. Biv (R.O.Y.G.B.I.V.), represented each color of the rainbow (e.g., R for red, O for orange). Until this day, I can recall that doll and the colors of the rainbow in their proper order.

Here, Catch!

When learning the names of objects in French class, the teacher would toss the item (such as a banana) to a student and call out its French name. The student would then toss it back while, at the same time, saying the item's name. What could have been a boring vocabulary drill was made much more interesting.

Let George Do It

My high-school biology teacher used a skeleton, named "George," as his laboratory assistant and, of course, to show things about human anatomy. George was so popular that someone even tried to run him as a candidate for student government.

Off with His Head

My high school English teacher brought in a mini-guillotine and cut pieces of carrots and other vegetables when we studied *A Tale of Two Cities*. We cheered on the "executions," just like the citizens of Paris had done. The vegetable slices were distributed to students who continued to talk about the book well after class.

Pavlov's Dogs

Our psychology professor used a real lemon to demonstrate classical conditioning. You see the lemon and you begin to salivate, even though you may try to resist. On a different occasion, she announced that we were going to have a "pop-quiz." Faces flushed, heart beats increased, palms became sweaty — all at the mere mention of "pop-quiz." Classical conditioning was, once again, demonstrated.

Slinky

In science class, the teacher used a slinky to demonstrate how seismic waves move through different materials. For some reason, "seeing" the motion of the wave just made more sense than viewing the diagrams in the textbook. This same teacher used chemical "tinker toys" to teach us how to construct atoms and molecules. Having used these toys to demonstrate concepts in class, he bragged that he now could write the cost of them off on his income tax (another acting/teaching tool — humor).

THE MASTER'S VOICE

For further discussion of the concepts and skills presented in this chapter, read the following paragraphs in Appendix II: Testimonials from Award-Winning College Professors: Grimnes, 4; Hall, 2; Harrison, 3–7; Lavin and Lewis, 16, 17; Richardson, 3.

CHAPTER 10

SUSPENSE AND SURPRISE

It is by surprises that experience teaches all she designs to teach us.
— *Collected Papers of Charles Sanders Pierce*, Vol. V

INTRODUCTION

What common complaint do many students have about schools and classrooms today? "They are boring." Asked "What is boring?" students respond, "The teachers, the curriculum." What common complaint do many teachers — after the first several years' idealism has tarnished — have about teaching. "It is boring." Actually, teachers mask the word "boring" in such responses as, "The kids just don't respond; they don't show much of an interest," or "I get so tired of having to teach the same thing period after period, day after day." It is clear that teachers, too, are bored.

That all students and teachers at some time become bored is axiomatic. The introduction of suspense and surprise into teaching can help resolve this common complaint. According to Ramsell (1978, 22), "When we are reacting physically and emotionally to surprise, boredom cannot be part of that response." Both teachers and students have something to gain through the use of suspense and surprise.

CREATING THE TWO ELEMENTS

Although both elements, suspense and surprise, are included in this same chapter, there are differences between the two. Suspense is something that is developed over a period of time as the story or event unfolds. Intrigue, especially dramatic intrigue — whether on stage, in film, or in the classroom — helps develop this suspense. Creating intrigue, and hence suspense, is possible in physics (Why does the earth stay in an orbit around the sun?), in mathematics (What is the probability of at least two students in the same room of thirty having the same birthday?), or chemistry (What is "heavy" about heavy water?). Suspense is equally possible, and useful, in history (Why did Napoleon hold his hand inside his coat?) and literature (How did Tom Sawyer get his friends to help with the work of painting the fence?). With a little imagination, no subject matter is alien to suspense.

Surprise, on the other hand, is said to depend upon unexpected events or special effects (Comisky and Bryant 1982). "Surprise takes place when a student is presented with a phenomenon that violates expectations derived from existing beliefs" (Vidler and Levine 1981, 274). An expectation, first established, is challenged by a contradictory, unexpected event. Cognitive dissonance (Festinger 1957) (the theory that people experience tension when a belief is challenged by an inconsistent behavior) is created. Such a dissonance, when one gets what is not expected, is understood even by four-year-olds (MacLaren and Olson 1993).

But should an event or effect be totally unexpected? Murray (1984) argues that with surprise the "cart should come before the horse." We are much more likely to perceive surprise if we have reason to expect it. This sense of a shared surprise creates a shared experience helping to bond the audience and the actor—the students and the teacher.

> No surprise for the writer, no surprise for the reader.
> —Robert Frost

Suspense creates tension; surprise generates tension. This tension prompts us to attempt to resolve the dissonance, to explore further for answers, to ask "Why?" questions, and to search for cause-and-effect explanations. We are, in fact, motivated! Order is sought for unexplained events.

Both elements, suspense and surprise, are accompanied by physiological changes (e.g., rapid breathing, gasping air, flushed face), behavioral patterns (e.g., including distinct facial expressions), and subjective experiences (Meyer, Niepel, Rudolph, and Schutzwohl 1991). Suspense and surprise create an emotional impact upon students' senses, and "The more you involve your students' senses, the more you sharpen their ability to learn" (Wells 1979, 53).

THE UNPREDICTABLE REAL WORLD

Too often teachers teach as if the world were predictable. It isn't—or at least most of it isn't. The black-and-white world of clearly right answers and wrong answers is a fallacy. Poetry and literature are not predictable. Psychology and sociology are not predictable. Even mathematics and chemistry are not predictable. Ask any scholar in his or her field. They will tell you this is so. We don't know whether it is part of some grand plan or not, but the world, not just schools and classrooms, would be boring if total predictability prevailed.

How can suspense and surprise be used in schools? Lowman (1984) suggests that teachers should use the elements of suspense and surprise when they enter the classroom. After all, actors pay attention to this all-important, stage-setting, entrance. What successful entertainer would simply, without fanfare, walk onto a stage? Rock stars have their accompanying fireworks and smoke, live theater has its dimming of the house lights and the raising of the stage curtain, and Johnny Carson has his variations of "Here's Johnny!"

Although it is usually preferable for teachers to get to class well before its official starting time, a variance from this format can be "surprising" and "suspense-building" — "Where could the teacher be? It is almost time to start class." A teacher might also work on varying how he or she actually enters the room. Whereas predictability breeds contentment, the unexpected breeds attentiveness. One could burst into the room and, while rapidly walking to the front of the room, begin lecturing. Consider varying exits, too. Perhaps a colleague could step in at the end of the class and announce in that classic entertainer-exiting style, "(your name) has left the auditorium!"

Students would be better served if they were taught that the world is full of the unexpected — suspense and surprise. Not only would teachers' use of the unexpected, then, be a sound pedagogical tool; its use would reflect the reality of the world. Without the feelings of uncertainty and insecurity that accompany suspense and surprise, learners quickly fall into a state of complacency and overconfidence where unthinking approaches to problem-solving are mechanically applied. Unfortunately such an approach to problem-solving dominates many of today's classrooms.

Eureka!
— Archimedes

Step-by-step "recipe solutions" regularly are applied (and reinforced) to get results without thought occurring about either the process or the result. What high school chemistry lab exists today where students do much more than don a white coat and safety goggles, play scientist, and "discover" exactly what the instructor had intended to be discovered? Where is the "discovery"? Kelser (1988) recommends assigning experiments that give students unexpected — surprising — results. A fellow chemist, Chirpich (1977, 378), agrees that "it is good to include some experiments that are more dramatic and that arouse student curiosity." This is good advice for all subject areas.

STORYTELLING

One hears the water running. The camera pans toward the Bates Hotel bathroom where, silhouetted behind the curtain, the unsuspecting woman is taking a shower. One hand of the mystery intruder (Norman, played by Anthony Perkins) is shown raised, holding a long butcher knife. The other hand is about to grasp the shower curtain and rip it aside. Twenty-five years later, this scene from Alfred Hitchcock's thriller *Psycho* continues to create viewer suspense and surprise.

Then there is the campfire story of the young couple parked on lovers' lane. Steamed windows accompany some adolescent necking. The music on the radio is interrupted by an announcement, "An escaped murderer, nicknamed the 'hook' due to his having one artificial arm, is rumored to have been seen in the area. Beware." The frightened young couple quickly put the car in gear and speed away. Upon arriving at the young lady's home, the boy gets out and walks around the car planning gallantly to open the door for his girlfriend—only to find a bloody "hook" hanging on the passenger-side door handle! Do you have goose bumps?

Effective storytellers have long known the power and persuasion of using suspense and surprise. Storytellers are part and parcel of human existence. Whether gathered around a primitive campfire or a formal dining-room table, storytelling was, and in many societies continues to be, an important medium for the transfer of knowledge and skills. Then and now, storytellers teach.

Whether in film or on stage, a story is told. The audience, often purposefully deceived by the movie's or play's plot, waits with anticipation to see "who done it." Suspense and surprise are often used to grab, as well as hold, the attention of the audience. Did the butler really do it? Will the damsel in distress be saved? Will the roadrunner ever be caught by the coyote? What is the big secret in the movie *The Crying Game*? In *Dallas*, who really shot J.R.? Tune in next season.

In the classroom, teachers can infuse their presentations with suspense. They can create a sense of dramatic tension and excitement that comes from expecting something important or unusual (Lowman 1984). Lectures can be delivered as if a story were being told. The excitement of discovering an unfolding plot, using only "clues" that have been dropped along the way, can heighten student suspense. Teachers can act as if they, too, are just now discovering the plot. They can share in the students' suspense.

According to Lowman (1984, 92): "Superb lecturers share many qualities with storytellers. They, too, save the conclusions or most crucial points until the end, having teased the students along the way with preliminary findings or interpretations. . . . [A]lmost any instructor can learn to be a good storyteller if he or she relaxes inhibitions and reacts to the suspense inherent in most content."

Watch the eyes of a child sparkle with anticipation at the parent's or teacher's opening line during story hour, "Once upon a time . . ." No matter how many times the line is used, the effect is the same. The child is excited about the unexpected. The child is spellbound. Watch a high school or college student's face as she wonders what the author means in the opening lines of the novel *A Tale of Two Cities*: "It was the best of times; it was the worst of times." How can it be the "best" and "worst" of times at the same time? The apparent discrepancy is surprising.

RELATIONSHIP TO OTHER ACTING SKILLS

Almost anything teachers do that is seen by students to be out of the ordinary will be viewed with curiosity. Therefore, each of the other acting/teaching skills highlighted in this book, if not part of a teacher's usual repertoire of behaviors, has the potential for creating suspense and surprise.

Unexpected animation in voice — perhaps a shout (surprise), perhaps a whisper (suspense) — can do the trick. Animation in body, possibly conveyed through sudden demonstrative body movements, can create both surprise and suspense. Greeting students on a Monday morning after having unexpectedly moved their desks into a new seating pattern might do it. Students wonder, "Gee, what's up?" A teacher playing a role, complete with supportive props (e.g., costumes), can be surprising and heighten suspense. Content-related humor, delivered at just the right moment, can be surprising. Teachers should keep their eyes open for opportunities to evoke suspense and surprise when using other acting/teaching skills.

BRINGING SUSPENSE AND SURPRISE INTO THE CLASSROOM

Although not intended to be a definitive list of suggestions, the following do represent a variety of ways in which suspense and surprise can be brought into the classroom. In those circumstances where the suggestions appear content-specific, use your imagination to envision how the basis of the suggestion could be used in other subject areas.

- Do not always announce to students what activities will take place during the class period. Let each activity, revealed one at a time like the layers of an onion, help create suspense and surprise.
- Use self-disparaging comments in moderation. Before doing so, one should have a healthy rapport with students. Mild self-disparaging comments, not the Rodney Dangerfield "I get no respect" variety, are unexpected in the students' experience. Students find it surprising to hear teachers "pick" on themselves

for a change. Skillful teachers exploit their own fallibility (Rubin 1985).

- Feign mistakes. Rubin (1985, 135) argues that students "are delighted when a normally accurate teacher makes a mistake." They are surprised. The use of a feigned reaction is "neither deceptive nor dishonest in spirit when the purpose is altruistic." Aware of this, enterprising practitioners occasionally engage in a bit of "planned error." The teacher could accompany this error with an exaggerated display of consternation or despair. The more the teacher "hams it up," the more surprising it is. Students, then, can be asked to help correct the error—a useful, but surprising, pedagogical tool.

- Feign laryngitis. A professor whom we know feigned laryngitis on the day that a wrap-up discussion was scheduled for an earlier off-campus, field experience. In an uncharacteristic fashion, the discussion was dominated by students. All the teacher could do was gesture and, perhaps, scribble boldly on the chalkboard, "Tell us more." "Why is that?" "What about such and such?" Imagine the students' surprise when, while leaving the classroom at the end of an exciting class, the instructor said, in a clear voice, "I will see each of you on Wednesday."

- Provide students with the opportunity for meaningful guessing—call it forming hypotheses if you like—before solving or presenting solutions (Johnson 1973). The anticipation associated with guessing "who done it" or "what color the powder will turn the solution" heightens the suspense.

- Use "what-if" exercises. A what-if exercise asks students to extrapolate information, to go beyond what is known for sure and venture into the suspense of the unknown. What if the Germans had won World War II? What if ice did not float? What if we reduce by half the size of the House of Representatives? What if people were regularly to live to over one-hundred years old? Today's computer spreadsheets (e.g., Lotus 1-2-3) allow us to play what-if games with numbers, such as the return expected for different proposed interest rates. Every discipline has a past and a future. Both are ripe for surprising what-if exercises.

- Use an accomplice. In an administration of justice course, one instructor had a primed student burst into the classroom, "shoot" him with a water pistol, and then quickly exit—not the usual classroom experience. Students were then asked to describe the perpetrator. Few could do so accurately. The lecture on the reliability and validity of eyewitness testimony followed.

- Bait students. Ask students to do something that, although it appears possible, can't be done. For instance, using a bull's-eye target, teach students the concepts of "Validity" and "Reliability." Tell the students that you are testing a rifle's validity and reliability. Pretend that you have five shots to fire at a bull's-eye target (figure 10.1). Show the students what a "Reliable" and "Valid" pattern of shots would look like—all five shots closely (reliably) grouped in the bull's eye (valid). Ask them to create shot patterns for the three remaining combinations. Looks easy, but it is impossible to do. There is no way to have a pattern of shots that are "Valid" and "Not Reliable." By definition, all things that are valid are reliable! Surprising? Yes! Remembered? Yes!

Figure 10.1
Bull's-Eye Target

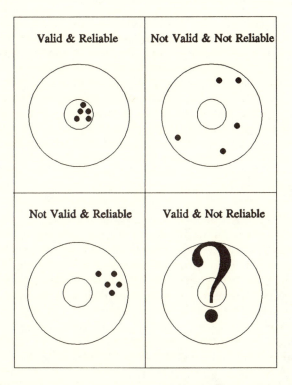

- Still another version of baiting is telling students enough of a story, or revealing enough of an event, to pique their curiosity. "Once baited, the audience wants to find out who wins, who loses, whether the villain receives his just deserts" (Rubin 1985, 113). One of the authors teaches Thomas Gordon's *T.E.T.: Teacher Effectiveness Training*, Roadblocks to Communication. When introduced to these twelve roadblocks, students realize that they unknowingly use them all the time. Just when the students are begging to know what alternative behaviors they could use, the instructor announces, "Sorry, but we are out of time. We will have to wait until tomorrow to find out about Gordon's alternatives." Healthy suspense is created, perhaps not so different from the Saturday morning serial episodes that made you wait until the following week to see how things turned out.

- Start the class off with a surprising behavior or event. We know of one methods teacher who, about to lecture on the subject of discrimination to his sociology students, walks to the door, as if someone has hailed him from the hall, and screams in a booming voice at that person, "What do you mean I am prejudiced? Some of my best friends are Black!" After an uncomfortable pause, he screams, "What do you mean I am prejudiced? Some of my best friends are Jews." Surprising behavior for Professor X? Yes. At this point students begin to suspect something is up. The professor asks students what goes through their minds when they hear such statements. The universal response is that the screamer must, in fact, be prejudiced. Otherwise, why would he protest so much? The lecture continues. Everyone is paying attention.

- Display a prop that is destined for later use and let students wonder about its use until later in the class period. Who would not experience a feeling of suspense if a teacher walked into class, placed a paper bag (obviously full of something) in a prominent place, and then proceeded to "ignore" it? It would have our curiosity piqued. Suspense, and possibly surprise, is created.

SUMMARY

Listed among a handful of components for teachers' success, House highlights one of the "S's" in the word *success* as surprise. She describes the personal feelings of "renewed awe and wonder and surprise" (1988, 640) that she experiences when studying her disciplines of science and mathematics. These same feelings, we believe, are shared with most successful teachers in any subject area. The trick is for teachers to convey this sense of suspense and surprise to students.

"People seem to enjoy being placed in suspense" (Zillmann and Hay 1975, 308). This fact is evident from the earliest measures psychologists made of kindergarten children where the children expressed a clear preference for story-liking based upon a suspense theme (Jose and Brewer 1990). Whether it is Hitchcock's classic *Rear Window* or Spielberg's thriller *Raiders of the Lost Ark*, it is clear that theater and film directors know and exploit this fact. Although teachers cannot be expected, especially on a daily basis, to present such attractive themes of good and evil forces (e.g., man-versus-man, man-versus-nature), teachers can capitalize on those opportunities that do exist.

THROUGH THE STUDENTS' EYES

When surveyed regarding the use of suspense and surprise in the classroom, students offered real-life examples such as those that follow. Although each example refers to the use of suspense and surprise in a particular subject area, the application to other disciplines is evident.

Paper Drive

For two weeks, Mrs. A., my high school English teacher, asked us to bring in all of our old newspapers from home. We didn't have the slightest idea why we were doing this. Finally, she broke the suspense and told us to divide into groups of three, use our creativity, and "make" something from *Beowulf*, a topic we had been studying for the past week. Our group made a huge model of Grendel. I think the activity was a good stress-breaker for the class.

Blindfolded

For composition class, we would do a composition describing something with one of our senses. Then that sense would be blocked. For instance, we would be blindfolded and asked to describe what was put into our hands, on our tongues, and under our noses.

Duck!

When lecturing about making observations in science, Mr. M. proved that you can't always rely on seeing-is-believing. To prove this point, he showed us a good-sized rock, which he then threw at a student. The student ducked to escape the rock, which turned out to be simply a hunk of styrofoam.

Is the Principal Coming?

To help us learn the metric system, Mr. A. brought in his electric jigsaw and actually cut a wooden meter stick into important lengths (e.g., centimeter, decimeter). To say the least, we were surprised. He even "posted a guard" in the hall to watch out for the principal (suspense). Because it looked as if we were getting away with something, everyone paid attention. Each student was given a length of the meter stick (a prop) and was required to have it with him at all times and be prepared to produce it upon demand.

ESP

My psychology teacher fooled the class (a little bit of role-playing) by claiming to be able to communicate with a colleague with extrasensory perception (ESP). He did it so convincingly that, upon revealing the purpose of the activity, we were surprised at how easily all of us were fooled.

Soap Bubbles

Our engineering teacher gave us the problem of connecting the cities of Boston, Chicago, New Orleans, Atlanta, Spokane, and San Diego with the least amount of concrete (shortest path) possible. A complicated problem? Not really. The surprisingly easy solution was to place pegs (representing the cities) between two pieces of plexiglass and, when dipped in a soap solution, the resulting soap film connected the pegs with minimum surface area — hence distance — possible. Amazed is a better word than surprised.

THE MASTER'S VOICE

For further discussion of the concepts and skills presented in this chapter, read the following paragraphs in Appendix II: Testimonials from Award-Winning College Professors: Carroll, 2–5; Hall, 6; Light, 3; Lisska, 3–7; Mahoney, 2; McBrayer, 4, 5.

PART III

EPILOGUE

CHAPTER 11

BEHIND THE SCENES

A professor can never better distinguish himself
in his work than by encouraging a clever pupil.
—Linnaeus

INTRODUCTION

In this chapter, we present, not a "tool" that the teacher can borrow from the
actor, but rather a reminder. An actor is vividly aware that the performance
seen by the audience is a mere fraction of the work involved in staging a
play. It is an *important* fraction, but still a fraction. The bulk of the work
happens "behind the scenes." That is the reminder for teachers: most of the
work that makes the classroom come alive happens behind the scenes.

For an actor, the "behind the scenes" category includes endless hours of
personal preparation as well as the coordinated contributions of a large
support crew who attend to the staging issues of lights, sound, props, and
so on. Without that background preparation by all parties, the performance
itself would be of very poor quality, no matter how great the actor's
presentational skills.

Likewise for the teacher, "behind the scenes" refers both to personal
preparation and to preparing the accoutrements of the performance with the
help of some support staff. When one thinks of preparation in regard to
teaching, content mastery is probably what comes to mind. Content mastery
certainly is vital, but it has been amply treated elsewhere. In this instance,
preparation refers to preparing for the *act* of teaching, not preparing the
subject matter per se. Such preparation requires attention to the teacher's
"spirit," if you will, and to the "things" of the stage called a classroom.

INTERNAL PREPARATION

Richard Weaver, the noted communication scholar, asserts that the
problem with college teaching is that so few faculty have a "passion" for

teaching (Weaver 1981). His position is shared by many others, including students. If the faculty member sees the teaching task as simply a job, it will be impossible to generate the enthusiasm necessary to perform it well. All that has been suggested in this book regarding the tools of teaching is valueless if used by a mere technician. The user must be an artist—one for whom the teaching-learning process is anticipated joyfully and executed with dedication.

Another scholar reminds us that the etymology of the word "professor" is the reference to a person able to make a profession of faith in the midst of a dangerous world (Palmer 1990). Seen from this angle, then, to be a professor requires some courage of conviction. One must be willing to present the issues, the ideas, the challenges, whether students are motivated to listen or not. It is the professor's task to create that motivation by allowing his/her *passion* for the subject matter and for the teaching-learning process to be evident.

Recapturing that passion is what internal preparation is all about. Like actors, teachers must feel a commitment to express themselves before going on stage. That commitment is what gives teachers self-confidence. In the midst of the pressures of "outcomes-based assessments," performance reviews, troubled students, funding shortages (the list goes on and on), teachers must remind themselves why they got into the business of teaching. It is the magic of learning, the challenge to make a difference, the wonder of knowledge. Do these sound familiar? Every teacher who can recapture that passion within is prepared to handle the tools and techniques of the classroom.

One master teacher even suggests that just prior to each class taught, the teacher should pause for a moment to prepare emotionally for entering the classroom (Lowman 1984). In that moment, the teacher should clear his or her mind of extraneous issues, review the plan for this day's lesson and recommit himself or herself to the challenge of the teaching-learning process.

That sort of mental preparation is exactly what most great actors do just before taking the stage. It is a habit that transfers well to the theater of the classroom.

EXTERNAL PREPARATION

By external preparation, we are referring to the preparation of the artifices that will be needed for the performance, be it on the stage or in the classroom. Working behind the scenes in the theater are a myriad of support crews making costumes, planning makeup, constructing sets, procuring or creating props, and designing light and sound systems for the production. These elements are important to the performance, planned in conjunction with consideration of the actors, but not part of the actors per se — thus the descriptor: external preparation. Similar preparation ought to be addressed by teachers.

Once teachers have decided to incorporate some dramaturgical devices into their teaching, they should start finding items for their prop locker. This is more or less a "hope chest" of prop and costume items the teachers think may be useful for some future lessons as well as those that they need immediately.

If the teacher has decided to use props, costumes, special lighting, or any other kind of "staging," help should be sought in locating suitable free materials for the prop locker before deciding to invest any money in purchasing the items. The college or school custodial staff may be your best source of knowledge about what materials are lying around the buildings that could be used, for instance. Naturally, the theater department would be another good resource.

If teachers must go shopping, they should start with yard sales. We earlier referred to one successful professor's two-hat technique. That professor reports that he has gathered most of his hats from yard sales and junk stores. Either he has purchased them himself or others, knowing of his teaching style, will pick up some unique hat for him that they happen to run across (Duncombe and Heikkinen 1988). Such a network of friends is the teacher's costume or prop crew. It's not Agnes De Mille, but it is still a very fruitful resource "behind the scenes."

What we have just been describing is the external preparation to generate the "things" needed by the teacher for such acting techniques as role-playing and use of props. The other acting techniques also require considerable work behind the scenes, but of a less tangible nature.

As previously noted, the teacher seeking to use certain acting devices will need to build a repertoire of sorts. Included may be humorous cartoons, striking anecdotes, creative ideas for rearrangement of classroom space, great opening lines, and more. Building one's acting/teaching repertoire should be an ongoing process.

Any time teachers feel themselves going a little stale, they should check their repertoire for innovative ideas they may have stored away for just such an occasion and have forgotten about. Most teachers can attest that creative ideas come at the most inopportune times. So a teacher's file may include notes jotted on napkins, concert programs, airline ticket folders, or grocery lists. Teachers should make notes whenever ideas come to mind, file them, and check back on them periodically.

As has been stressed by numerous pedagogical scholars, good teaching results from good planning: setting goals and objectives and selecting strategies for accomplishing them (Eison 1990). But, as is learned from the field of acting, those strategies won't simply become apparent, nor are there any resource manuals listing all available strategies so that a strategy may just be selected. Instead, an active repertoire of personally suitable strategies must be developed. A huge list of possible strategies to choose from may be generated by jotting down instructional techniques that are heard, read, or suddenly pop into a teacher's head. This is external preparation that requires no significant time or a support crew; it just takes thinking ahead.

SUMMARY

What the students see and hear from a good teacher at class time is the tip of the iceberg. In order for the performance that is a class to be successful, the teacher will have invested time and effort behind the scenes. Like the actor, the teacher may have enlisted the support of other crew members or may have relied on his/her own resources. Either way, the teacher will have prepared the materials needed for effective presentation of the day's subject and will have prepared emotionally by gearing up to be "on stage."

THE MASTER'S VOICE

For further discussion of the concepts and skills presented in this chapter, read the following paragraphs in Appendix II: Testimonials from Award-Winning College Professors: Soenksen, 2, 4.

CHAPTER 12

CLASSROOM MANAGEMENT

The discipline of colleges and universities is in general contrived, not for the benefit of the students, but for the interest, or more properly speaking, for the ease of the masters.

—Adam Smith

INTRODUCTION

How do acting skills and classroom management fit together? It would not be surprising if, while you were reading previous chapters, you had already given some thought to how acting skills might contribute to more effective classroom management. To help broaden your thoughts on this subject, we offer several specific applications of how acting skills can contribute to more effective classroom discipline.

CLASSROOM SPACE

One of the authors had a teacher named Brother Shad, at least that is what everyone called him. He was a very old English teacher who never got up from his desk. Students thought, due to his movement limitations about the room, that they — especially those in the back of the room — would be able to get away with murder. Wrong! Brother Shad had lined the sides and back of his room with photographs of past classes, allowing students' movements and antics to be clearly reflected in the mirror-like glass covering the photographs. He could see all. He, like any good actor or teacher, had planned his use of space carefully! He had done his work "behind the scenes."

A recognized ingredient of successful classroom management is possessing "withitness," as Kounin (1970) calls it. Being "withit" means knowing what is going on at all times — knowing who is doing what, when, and where. Effective use of classroom space, one of our acting/teaching skills, can help teachers be "withit."

Proxemics, a topic discussed in the chapter on Classroom Space, has its classroom management equivalent — proximity control.   It is easy to understand that students are less likely to misbehave when a teacher is standing close to them. It should be of no surprise to anyone that mischief-makers try to keep as much distance as possible between themselves and their teachers. Effective use of classroom space can thwart such students.

A teacher's presence can be made known to students who are seated farthest away, even when it is inconvenient, or even impossible, to be physically next to them. This can be done by carrying on some sort of running "joke" or good-hearted bantering with students seated in the back rows.   Best done before class or just as class starts, such behaviors demonstrate that the teacher is tuned in ("withit") to the far reaches of the classroom. In a raised lecture hall, the professor might ask, "Just checking, is the oxygen too thin that high up?" While announcing the assignment for tomorrow, the teacher might stop part way through and, as if on a sound stage, ask for sound check: "Am I coming through loud and clear back there?"

Creative use of classroom space in the form of reducing the distance between a teacher and students, moving students and/or the teacher, or creating more accessible paths or aisles can all contribute to more effective classroom management. But effective use of classroom space is not the only acting/teaching skill relevant to classroom management.

ANIMATION IN BODY

Another acting-related skill that is effective in establishing and maintaining classroom management is animation in body — actually, *lack* of animation in body. Jones, in his book *Positive Classroom Discipline* (1987), stresses the value of remaining totally inanimate. He recommends that teachers practice, and then deliver, their best "boy am I absolutely bored" look in response to students who are misbehaving. It takes the wind right out of their sails.

He recommends that teachers think of their dirty laundry or some other boring chore, make slow (but deliberate) turns in the direction of the perpetrator, take two deep breaths before saying anything (thus not appearing startled), and hang their hands and arms limp at their sides (not crossed in front their chest or provocatively set on their hips).   The nonverbal message to the student is clear: "Your antics are pretty boring. Ho, hum. Are you through yet?"

Jones (1987) describes a hierarchial series of limit-setting teacher behaviors for students who range from what he calls "penny-ante gamblers" to "high-rollers." All involve little or no animation on the part of the teacher. A minimum of talking, too, is suggested. Jones' limit-setting behaviors, in order of seriousness, all involve teachers swinging into *inaction*!

Whether lecturing or moving about the room helping students, when a teacher spots a misbehaving student, immediate action (inaction) is warranted. Jones (1987) suggests using, among other tactics, The Look, Moving In, and Palms and Prompt.

The Look

Turn around fully, in a regal fashion, and face the disruptive student

Make good eye contact

Relax (two relaxing breaths)

Say the student's first name loud enough to be heard

Relax (two relaxing breaths)

Wait (look bored; figure 12.1). This provides time for the student to decide to behave.

Moving In (if required)

Same as above, but now walk (slowly and deliberately) to the edge of the student's desk (legs just touching edge of desk)

Relax (two relaxing breaths)

Wait, maintain eye contact (look bored — really bored)

When student returns to the designated task for at least fifteen seconds, lean over and offer a sincere "Thank you"

Move Out — return to where you were originally in the room

Turn and watch the student (two relaxing breaths)

Palms and Prompt (if required)

Same as above, but now place palms flat on student's desk. In doing so, the teacher now has even closer eye contact with the student

Relax (two relaxing breaths)

Prompt the student by telling him or her exactly what you want to be done

Wait, maintain eye contact (look bored — really, really bored)

When student returns to the designated task for at least fifteen seconds, lean over and offer a sincere "Thank you"

Move Out — Return to where you were originally in the room

Turn and watch the student (two relaxing breaths).

Although some of these behaviors may seem, at first, to be unnatural, the more a teacher practices these actions (e.g., looking bored, turning in a regal fashion) the more genuine they will appear to students. After all, isn't

Figure 12.1
Teacher Looking Bored

Drawing courtesy of Mark Fisher.

this exactly what an actor or actress must do when asked to play a challenging role—practice and practice until his or her actions become believable to an audience?

The teacher's calm and business-like manner (at least it should appear that way on the outside) denies students the attention they are craving through such misbehavior (Dinkmeyer, McKay, and Dinkmeyer, Jr. 1980). Calmness displays confidence; willingness to take the time to deal with the problem reveals commitment; proximity reinforces intensity. These three ingredients, heightened through successful acting, almost guarantee results.

The power of using nonverbal messages needs to be stressed. These behaviors can be a nonoffensive (safe) means of reminding others who it is that possesses greater power and higher status. Nonverbal behaviors "associated with dominance include eye contact (even staring), relaxed but not slumped posture, expressive and expansive gestures, touch initiation, classic clothing and personal artifacts, expansive use of space, and poised, straightforward posture" (Andersen 1986, 48). More experienced teachers use these dominance-expressive behaviors; less experienced teachers tend to behave in nonverbally submissive ways. These two sets of behaviors convey two distinct images. It takes just a moment or so for students to note the difference.

While the emphasis in the above paragraph is on stopping inappropriate behavior, nonverbal behaviors can also be used to start or encourage appropriate behavior. Smiling, eye contact, nodding, and supportive gesturing—at the right moment—are among the nonverbal responses teachers can offer that are likely to heighten desired student interaction. These behaviors signal that the teacher is interested in what the student is saying. Stimulating student interaction can be further encouraged by another example of teacher inaction—using a pause. Ten to fifteen seconds of a well-placed pause can do wonders to stimulate participation.

SUSPENSE AND SURPRISE

Suspense and surprise are acting skills that can contribute directly to improved classroom management. Go out of your way to learn good things about your students: their work in other classes, family, part-time jobs, efforts and accomplishments in sports, participation in extracurricular activities, for instance. Actually, this is not very difficult, and even less time-consuming, to do. Just keep your eyes and ears open. Try talking with fellow faculty; try reading the school newspaper.

Armed with a knowledge of these "good" things, set about to surprise students by "dropping" the news when they least expect it. At the beginning of your class, you could say, "Joe, looks like you really had quite a soccer game on Saturday," "Wendy, that was a creative way in which you helped organize the food drive for the homeless shelter," or "Bill, how does it feel to be the only one to get a perfect paper in Mr. Sands' class?" Don't dwell on any one item. That's not the point. Don't give students the time to think how you know what you know. Just "drop" the bit of surprise information, and go on with the scheduled lesson.

The effect of delivering this unexpected (surprising) information is twofold (Tauber 1990). First, it conveys to your students that you are tuned into their lives beyond merely what they are doing in your class. This helps teachers develop what French and Raven (1960) call referent power—a sense of common purpose, one person identifying with another. Two, it keeps students "on their toes" as they wonder *how* you seem to know so much about them. They start to think that if you know this information, maybe you are also in a position to know when they might be trying to get away with something. You come off as being someone who must have eyes and ears everywhere.

HUMOR

The use of humor, too, impacts upon classroom management. When humor is used as a supplement to, and not a substitute for, teaching, its most positive benefits to classroom management come forth. Effective use of humor reinforces the teacher's superior position in the classroom. Psychologists recognize that it is "the superior that most often uses humor in communication with the inferior" (Vizmuller 1980, 266). In this context, the words "superior" and "inferior" are not derogatory terms; they simply specify status or position.

A recognition by the students of a teacher's higher status enables that teacher to use French and Raven's (1960) legitimate power (authority granted someone due to their position) more effectively. Students, too, recognize the confidence that accompanies a teacher's successful use of humor. The belief is that only a confident, in-control teacher would risk using humor.

In addition to these comments regarding the general use of humor, there are endless examples of specific applications of humor that can affect classroom discipline. A subject-matter-related riddle, funny story, or pun seems to have the power to capture a learner's attention regardless of age, gender, grade level, or subject.

For instance, a riddle can initiate some healthy competition to be the first (individual or group) to figure it out. Directed competition is healthy; it is productive. It can channel, in a constructive way, students' need to compete. The funny story or pun can create a shared experience. People sharing a common experience are more likely to feel part of a group and, as a result, less likely to do something to damage it, that is, misbehave.

SUMMARY

The common ingredient in all acting skills that can contribute to classroom management is their impact upon perceived teacher enthusiasm which, in turn, secures students' attention and holds their interest. A paper bag—containing something—that the teacher has placed in a prominent location and the suspense it elicits can grab students' attention that might otherwise be directed elsewhere. Finding the mathematics teacher dressed in a short-order cook's outfit, role-playing as Jamie Escalante did in *Stand and Deliver*, would hold most students' interest that might otherwise have been misdirected.

A teacher's animation in voice (i.e., a whisper) can have significant attention-getting power, possibly diverting students's temptation to chit-chat with a neighbor and thus cause a disturbance. Moving the front of the room to the back, through the simple operation of writing on the "back" (now front) board makes surprising use of classroom space. Students hiding in the back are now right there in the front. And so go the many examples that can be offered.

Teachers who incorporate acting skills into their teaching will be better able to secure students' attention and maintain their interest. Plain and simple—attentive and interested students are less likely to misbehave.

CHAPTER 13

CONCLUSION

The shrewd guess, the fertile hypothesis, the courageous leap to a tentative conclusion — these are the most valuable coin of the thinker at work.
— Bruner

WHERE TO TURN FOR HELP

Good teaching practice is out there. So states a recent vice-president of the American Society for Training and Development. But educators are not utilizing the best practices (Mark 1989). As we have argued throughout this book, part and parcel of this "good practice" is making better use of acting skills in the classroom. Among the assumptions held regarding the teaching-learning process, Rubin (1985, 100) believes that "even the dullest of subjects can be taught in a way that intrigues the learner." But how is this sense of intrigue generated? It's likely that the teacher used "something dramatic, imaginative, bewitching" (Wells 1979, 53).

Teachers can find help in books on practical tips such as Magnan's (1989). He advocates, among other tips, "Think of it as 'show' business (more 'show' and maybe a little less 'tell,'" "Think BIG" (the value of eye contact, projecting the voice, using gestures larger than life), "People your ideas," and "Return with your students to the people and places and time that gave us the knowledge we want to transfer," and "Claim your territory" (deliver points loud and clear from the front; move out among students to elaborate or illustrate points).

We can also turn to other printed resources such as those produced by faculty development offices, especially those at larger institutions. For instance, our university produces and distributes *The Penn State Teacher* to all new faculty. This resource, a collection of readings and practical advice for beginning teachers (Enerson and Plank 1993), offers, among many other tips, "Don't be afraid to use humor," "An effective lecture has a certain dramatic quality . . . many people find it useful to draw a comparison between lecturing and acting," and "Make use of devices (i.e., props)."

Teachers can also turn to Konstantin Stanislavski, the Soviet director, whose proven methods of teaching drama serve as the bible for many

Introduction to Acting 101 instructors. Travers and Dillon (1975), in *The Making of a Teacher*, suggest using Stanislavski's model to train teachers as performing artists.

Teachers or professors can profit from reading journal articles, especially those written by our peers, attesting to the value of and explaining how to incorporate acting skills. One easy way to locate such articles is to do a search of ERIC (Educational Resources Information Center), a government-funded CD-ROM data base which is available in most college and university libraries (see chapter 3). ERIC's clearinghouses are listed in Appendix I: Sixteen ERIC Clearinghouses. The majority of ERIC users will be pleasantly surprised at the number of articles on the use of acting skills that they are able to locate.

Department heads and curriculum/supervision coordinators also are advised to conduct an ERIC search. In their case, they should look for articles that are subject-matter specific (e.g., engineering, English, psychology), as well as articles that are applicable to all subject areas. As heads or supervisors, they can then funnel relevant articles to those faculty to whom the material best applies. This could be the beginnings of a productive staff-development program.

Colleagues and those in the community who already possess acting skills are also a useful resource. People such as Robert Keiper (see chapter 3) at Western Washington University who offers a popular acting/teaching course, and Linc Fisch from Lexington, Kentucky, who, as a retired professor, not only conducts workshops and seminars on acting skills, but also develops "trigger films" — three- or four-minute films used to trigger audience/classroom discussions — immediately come to mind.

Then there is Bill Harrison, from Santa Rosa Junior College in California, who, with a background in theater and education, conducts an "Acting Techniques in Teaching" workshop for both basic- and higher-education audiences. W. Kaye Robinson, from Grand Canyon University in Arizona, also comes to mind. From work begun in her doctoral dissertation, she developed a course, "Dramatic Arts for Teachers," that helps education majors gain confidence in using dramatic behaviors. There also is Alan Friedman from Belleville Area College in Illinois who offers a half- or full-day workshop titled, "The Teacher as Actor," where he identifies and trains teachers in developable skills useful to both teachers and actors.

High school and college drama teachers can be contacted and asked to provide some inservice training. Community theater directors might be willing to provide some assistance. No doubt these people would be flattered that you have come to them for help. As resource people, these individuals are in a position to help teachers and professors take those first tentative steps into the world of acting — acting as it applies to teaching. And, unlike book and journal resources, these people are also in a position to provide feedback as you work at perfecting these acting skills.

A TEACHER'S MANNER AND METHOD

As the authors of this book, we want to acknowledge that we are teachers first and scholars second. Teaching is taken very seriously at our institution — so much so that every teacher has every class evaluated every semester. Merit pay, tenure, and promotion all are influenced by these results. The formal instrument used to collect data is called a Student Rating of Teacher Effectiveness (SRTE) form. When our students report, in anecdotal form, that "the professor was able to make an otherwise boring subject interesting," we are torn between competing reactions. One part of us wants to grab the students, shake them, and announce in no uncertain terms that, in fact, our subject is inherently interesting. Another side of us recognizes that perhaps we have accomplished just what we have set out to do — we have begun to turn students on to our subject areas. Time will tell.

"When we look back on our schooling, we remember teachers rather than courses — we remember their manner and method, their enthusiasm and intellectual excitement, and their capacity to arouse delight in, or curiosity about, the subject taught" (Hook 1981, 24). This "manner and method" reflects many of the acting strategies presented in this book that can, and should, be used by teachers.

Of all dramatic elements, says Klein (1990), characters and their dramatic actions are recalled more strongly and frequently than dialogue. We remember more about what people do than what they say. "Even more so than an actor, a teacher is a sculptor in snow" (Hook 1981, 24). Like the snow sculpture that will melt in the warming sun, the memories of a great teacher are preserved only by those who have *seen* him or her in action. The strategies presented in this book, then, may be even more important to a teacher than they are to an actor!

When asking what are the three most important ingredients to ensuring a successful retail business, most people are surprised with the answer, "Location, location, location." Robinson (1993), in her course, Dramatic Arts for Teachers, believes that teachers' success in the classroom is dependent upon "Performance, Performance, Performance." We hope that by reading this book teachers will perform, perform, perform — in the very best sense. We hope they will begin developing their unique, yet effective, "manner and method" acting skills.

APPENDIX I

SIXTEEN ERIC CLEARINGHOUSES

Adult, Career, and Vocational Education
Ohio State University
Center for Research in Vocational Education
1900 Kenny Road
Columbus, Ohio 43210-1090
(614) 292-4353
(800) 848-4815

Assessment and Evaluation
Catholic University of America
209 O'Boyle Hall
Washington, DC 20064-3893
(202) 319-5120
(800) 464-3742

Community Colleges
University of California at
  Los Angeles
Mathematical Sciences Building
Room 8118
405 Hilgard Avenue
Los Angeles, California 90024-1564
(310) 825-3931
(800) 832-8256

Counseling and Student Services
Curry Building
University of North Carolina
1000 Spring Garden Street
Greensboro, NC 27412-5001
(919) 334-5100
(800) 414-9769

Disabilities and Gifted Education
Council for Exceptional Children
1920 Association Drive
Reston, Virginia 22091-1589
(703) 620-3660
(800) 328-0272

Educational Management
University of Oregon
1787 Agate Street
Eugene, Oregon 97403-5207
(503) 346-5043
(800) 438-8841

Elementary and Early Childhood Education
University of Illinois
805 West Pennsylvania Avenue
Urbana, Illinois 61801-4897
(217) 333-1386
(800) 583-4135

Higher Education
George Washington University
One Dupont Circle, N.W., Suite 630
Washington, DC 20036-1183
(202) 296-2597
(800) 773-3742

Information and Technology
Syracuse University
Huntington Hall, Room 030
Syracuse, New York 13244-2340
(315) 443-3640
(800) 464-9107

Languages and Linguistics
Center for Applied Linguistics
1118 22nd St., N.W.
Washington, DC 20037-0037
(202) 429-9551
(800) 276-9834

**Reading, English, and
Communication**
Indiana University
Smith Research Center, Suite 150
2805 East 10th Street
Bloomington, Indiana 47408-2373
(812) 855-5847
(800) 759-4723

Rural Education and Small Schools
Appalachia Educational Laboratory
1031 Quarrier Street
P.O. Box 1348
Charleston, West Virginia 25325-1348
(304) 347-0400
(800) 624-9120

**Science, Mathematics, and
Environmental Education**
1929 Kenny Road
Columbus, Ohio 43210-1080
(614) 292-6717
(800) None available

**Social Studies/Social Science
Education**
Indiana University
Social Studies Development Center
Suite 120
2805 East 10th Street
Bloomington, Indiana 47405-2373
(812) 855-3838
(800) 266-3815

Teaching and Teacher Education
American Association of Colleges for
Teacher Education
One Dupont Circle, N.W., Suite 610
Washington, DC 20036-1186
(202) 293-2450
(800) 822-9229

Urban Education
Teachers College, Columbia
University
Institute for Urban and Minority
Education
Main Hall, Room 300, Box 40
525 West 120th Street
New York, New York 10027-9998
(212) 678-3433
(800) 601-4868

APPENDIX II

TESTIMONIALS FROM
AWARD-WINNING COLLEGE PROFESSORS

Testimonial 1
Gregory J. Baleja
Department of Business and Social Sciences
Alma College
Alma, Michigan 48801

(1) I have been involved in higher education for the past fourteen years, and during that time, I have often pondered why my teaching style has been so effective and well received by my students. I have taught at a variety of schools, ranging from large research-based universities to small liberal arts colleges. The schools' policies have varied from "open admissions" to "highly selective" admissions criteria. Since my evaluations have been consistent across the institutions, I am therefore forced to conclude that the success of my teaching style is *not* contingent on any one particular category of student.

(2) The question remains, why the success? Are there any common themes or practices that may account for this? In reviewing the comments sections of previous Instructor Evaluation Forms, and after a thorough self-evaluation, three areas are consistently noted: Voice Animation (Enthusiasm), Body Animation, and Subject Mastery. Each of these areas is expanded on below.

(3) First, the most consistent theme centers around the use of voice animation. This is especially true when it comes to the importance of "Enthusiasm." The following are some selected student (audience) comments regarding the importance of enthusiasm:

a. "_____ attacked this course with vigor and a sense of enthusiasm that is a necessity when dealing with the material presented in the course."

b. "_____ is an enthusiastic teacher. I have learned so much in this course. He is very good with the students. Teaches in an interesting and fair manner and it is obvious that he enjoys his work."

c. "Instructor was very enthusiastic and kept the attention of the class members well. Even when I was in my most exhausted state, he still had the ability to keep my attention. He was very well organized and knew what he was talking about."

d. "The Professor is enthusiastic and teaches in a manner which keeps the student's interest and encourages class participation. He is extremely well prepared for his lectures. He has a daily outline which aids students in their note taking."

(4) In order for the students to show enthusiasm for the subject matter, it is imperative for the instructor to do the same. In this day and age of entertainment, it is crucial for the professor to use a variety of vocal variation techniques. Just as a performer will use inflection in his/her voice to draw attention to a particular point in the narration, it is critical for professors to do the same. Inflections can be used to draw attention to a particular key point, or to reinforce various aspects of the lecture.

(5) Second, the use of body animation is important in gaining and then maintaining the attention of the audience (students). A professor standing in front of a podium or next to an overhead projector for an entire class period, creates a static environment that can lead to boredom and daydreaming, no matter how exciting the topic. Pacing the floor, talking with your hands, and the use of visual aids, for example, all lead to a dynamic environment within the classroom that prevents or at least minimizes the possibility of boredom. In addition, the professor needs to dress in a manner appropriate for the type of learning environment desired. Professional attire (two-piece suits, buttoned collar) creates an atmosphere of formality and superiority that may reduce interaction. Less formal attire (shirt and tie with open collar) may enhance the amount of interaction. Some student comments on this subject are listed below:

a. "Without the fear of an overpowering authority figure, I think we felt more comfortable in expressing our opinions."

b. "The open forum when discussing cases was very effective for it allowed *us* to think, and *you* to guide, instead of being *told* what to do."

(6) Communication and learning cannot take place if the receiver of the information either refuses to accept it or is unaware of its existence because of staring at the ceiling, daydreaming about some outside activity, or being put off by the formality of the class and professor.

(7) Finally, the professor needs to demonstrate mastery in the subject matter. This includes not only the normal knowledge associated with

subject mastery, but also the ability to communicate the information in a manner that the students are able to comprehend. The information must be presented in terminology the audience is familiar with. Also, the use of *current* real world examples will reinforce the importance of the concept and will help the student in retaining the information. The following are some examples of students' comments concerning this area:

a. "Examples used in class are very good and helped to illustrate points that could be boring and mundane."

b. "I felt the instructor made good use of examples which helped to make the course more interesting and easier to understand."

c. "Related concepts in class with examples of 'real world' very well so that we understood them better."

d. "The instructor *always* shows enthusiasm with every lecture. He has the distinct ability (which most teachers do not possess) to explain material with good examples that relate current aspects and learnings in other classes."

(8) Subject mastery is more than just theories and concepts. It also includes the ability to communicate the information in a manner that the audience understands and retains!

(9) In summary, many of the practices that have contributed to my success in the classroom can be directly correlated to some of the basic concepts and tenets of acting (subject mastery, voice, and body animation). In this TV age, it seems to be beneficial, if not a requirement, for a professor to be part entertainer (actor), in order to disseminate knowledge effectively and efficiently to the student population.

Testimonial 2
Stephen R. Borecky
Division of Natural Sciences
Carlow College
Pittsburgh, Pennsylvania 15213

(1) As I reviewed the draft of the table of contents for this book and tried to select the one or two specific areas to be addressed in this essay, I was reminded of a common question that is raised in my anatomy classes. Not a semester passes without one of my students asking, "What do you consider to be the most important organ system in the body?" My usual response centers on the concept of interrelatedness, since the survival of the organism as a whole depends upon the combined functions of all organs. I believe that the concept of interrelatedness also applies to the skills necessary for effective teaching. I am not suggesting that a weakness in or lack of one or

more of the specific skills discussed in this book automatically makes one an ineffective teacher, but I do feel that teaching effectiveness is greatly enhanced as new skills are acquired and others are modified and developed.

(2) I consider the development of teaching skills to be a gradual evolutionary process. Fish did not become amphibians and amphibians did not become reptiles in quantum leaps of anatomical and physiological changes, but rather evolved though a series of gradual changes influenced by the environment in which they lived. A similar pattern is observed in the evolution of teaching skills. However, unlike the random mutations associated with the evolution of animals, teachers can select and develop those traits that improve their performance within their own specific educational environments. Just as some traits are essential to the survival of organisms in any environment and others are unique specializations, there are teaching skills that must be mastered before entering any classroom setting and those that will slowly evolve to fit the teacher's personality and specific discipline. Subject mastery is one of those essential traits, but it has been my experience that this trait can produce conflicts in the development of other skills.

(3) Teachers at any academic level begin their careers as students and through course selections and research acquire the volumes of information that make them experts in their fields. Although familiarity with one's subject area is a vital component of quality teaching, it is equally important to develop those skills that separate the teacher from the lecturer. A lecture can be compared to reading a play, while teaching is the equivalent of viewing a stage performance. Both experiences provide the same information, but the performance makes the characters and plot come alive, and, if the actors have polished their skills, the audience comes away with a visual and auditory experience that they will remember. Teachers must avoid becoming so involved in learning the "lines" that the skills necessary for delivering them are neglected and a potentially dynamic learning experience becomes another "boring lecture" to the students.

(4) Familiarity with the subject can also result in a decline in enthusiasm as the same content material is presented year after year. At this time it is important to identify with the students in the class and remember that to them the information represents a totally new experience. I have heard actors state that they strive to generate the same level of enthusiasm for a role in their one-hundredth performance as they did in their first. Even though the scenes and dialogue have been rehearsed and performed many times before, they recognize that it is a new event for the members of the audience. If an actor rushed through a scene or failed to develop a character's personality, assuming that the audience was already aware of the plot, I am sure that the reviews of the performance would be less than favorable. It is the same in teaching. The humor, animation, and

enthusiasm displayed by the teacher provide the framework for an enjoyable learning experience.

(5) When actors can no longer generate enthusiasm for a role, they can move on to assume other roles in new productions. Unfortunately, teachers are not afforded this luxury, but the teacher does have an advantage over the actor. An actor who tires of a role is limited in the adjustments that can be made in the portrayal of the character while still maintaining the continuity of the performance. Iago portrayed as a comic hero would definitely upset the balance of Othello. On the other hand, a teacher can assume many characters and utilize many techniques and still present the same content material to the students. If a topic begins to appear dry and uninteresting to you as a teacher, you can imagine how the students in your class will respond to your presentation. Both teachers and lecturers update the content of the lessons to include new ideas and theories, but the teacher also strives to refine the techniques used in the presentation of the information. As teachers, our audiences pay a high price for admission to our performances, and I firmly believe that at the conclusion of the course they should feel that they have received their money's worth.

Testimonial 3
Virginia Schaefer Carroll
English Department
Kent State University
East Liverpool, Ohio 43920

(1) Because I teach composition and literature to non-majors who usually resist — if not detest — the subject matter of all English courses, one of my objectives in each course is to make the subject more interesting and accessible. Many of the acting skills described in this book can be useful in engaging students in the course and focusing their attention on the major ideas or problems of a discipline. The technique that I find most useful, however, is the dramatic aside.

(2) In the pedagogical context, an aside means a turning away from the "text" of the class lecture or outline for the day and a turning toward the students themselves. To be dramatic, the aside must be seen as a clear interruption of the text, probably achieved by such stage techniques as changing the voice, physical space, expression, and pacing of delivery. As on the stage, an effective aside should be a well-integrated surprise, performed naturally and spontaneously in response to the audience. Also, no matter how entertaining the aside may be, the professor must achieve a smooth transition back to the text.

(3) My own use of such a technique began with my first teaching at the

university level, probably partly due to my age (twenty, at that time) and stature (fairly short—I'm one of those people whose driver's license reflects her actual weight but a slightly exaggerated height). I learned quickly that a well-timed, slightly prolonged pause riveted the students' attention, and that I could use that space effectively with an aside. Sometimes these asides were as startling as an actor's movements toward the audience in experimental theater: for example, during a particularly dry—but essential—review of argumentative structure, I might suddenly change face and place, make direct eye contact, and say "I know what you're thinking." I then glance around the classroom, and in exaggerated parody of my and their voices, guess the random thoughts and complaints of a range of students. Their surprised laughter suggests that my guesses about their responses are fairly accurate and that they are relieved to know I understand their difficulty with the subject matter.

(4) In recent years, I have been relying on this technique much more unobtrusively, but students come to recognize and enjoy the moments when I drop the script. One of the skills of composition is the development of an argument through specific examples—a challenge to those who want to fill their essays with platitudes and lovely abstractions. And the literature in many courses, such as Great Books, seems remote and inaccessible to the students. So I frequently pepper the lectures with asides as examples; these are usually spontaneous responses to something in the room, to an NPR report I heard on the drive to campus, to an issue facing the university or community, to some event from my own life, or even to an occurrence out the window (the Ohio River is conveniently located as a visual aid). Sometimes these asides take on the proportions of true digressions, lasting a few moments and conveyed dramatically. But often I deliver them at high speeds or mumbling audibly; students learn to pay attention or they miss most of the jokes.

(5) Such a technique is especially effective at the campus where I teach. Most of the students are the first in their families to attend college; their mean age is around twenty-seven, and the campus is 70% women. Many of these students seek a connection to what they are learning and struggle to see an intersection of English courses and their career paths. The technique of using asides seems to put students at ease with what they are hearing and what they are thinking; the students become more animated, spontaneous, and enthusiastic in their responses; they seem to trust themselves more in drawing conclusions from their own experiences, responses, and observations (an essential skill in critical thinking); and they overcome some of their resistance to the subject matter. It's also fun.

Testimonial 4
Raymond J. Clough
Department of Modern Languages
Canisius College
Buffalo, New York 14208

(1) In the mid-60s, as a young college teacher, I had the good luck one evening to hear the actor Vincent Price do a dramatic reading of Edgar Allan Poe's "The Tell-Tale Heart." It was a large auditorium, and Price was sitting in an over-stuffed armchair, a table at his side and a large book on his lap—no other decor. Bathed in the soft glow of a spotlight, he proceeded to enthrall the audience of perhaps one thousand people with a flawless and moving reading of Poe's classic story. No one budged; few coughed. Price held his audience spellbound for the entire reading. He used all the tricks of his trade—dramatic pauses, voice modulation and projection, crisp articulation. He scanned the audience, seemed to be speaking directly to each one of us. The effect was verbal alchemy.

(2) This was a great epiphany for me. That night I relearned the importance of something I had been taught in grammar school—elocution—which, as every actor knows, is essential to the theater. A teacher must likewise pay attention to training the voice, learning to project it and to develop a comfortable, natural delivery style. The effort will pay enormous dividends in the classroom where it is critical to communicate clearly with your audience.

(3) Price's performance that night also drove home to me the necessity of knowing materials cold, of having a sense of stage presence, and the importance of gestures. His glances at the book on his lap were merely for calculated effect. He knew the tale by heart, and, as the story built to its inexorable climax, he put the book aside to rise and slowly move forward to his audience, beating his breast rhythmically as he described *basso profundo* the heart pounding ever-louder under the floor boards. He was clearly feeding off our rapt attention, and we, in turn, were responding to his transcendence. Effective teaching is performance art also. Every class can and should be a dramatic event, and, if you are very lucky, every now and then when you and the audience are one, you will know why it is a very special calling.

(4) Good teaching is natural. It flows. It requires a sense of timing. It is very useful to move around the room, make your students follow you as you approach them, invade their space conspiratorially, confidentially, as if to share something special with them and then draw back, pulling their attention toward you. A class can, in a sense, be choreographed, and the effect can be dramatic. You have to know how, as the comics say, to work a room. This, of course, can be taught theoretically, but the skill is best learned and honed by trial and error.

(5) An effective teacher knows instinctively how to hold a class. He or she has great flexibility and can adjust teaching techniques to the situation at hand. When things go flat, a little self-deprecating humor, improvisation, or a set routine can save the day. Effective communication and teaching require feedback. Personally, I depend on my classes every day. I thrive on their interest, and I am challenged by their lethargy. When my students are "into it," and I know I am reaching them, I react. I become more animated, sometimes even outrageous, in my attempts to make the information more memorable.

(6) It is a truism that people learn in different ways. As far as possible, classes must be multisensorial — a shotgun approach. We sometimes forget, however, that people also learn at different rates. Just as there are many rehearsals before opening night in the theater, classroom material must be reviewed, the message highlighted, repeated before the students are asked to "perform publicly" on an exam.

(7) Good teaching must constantly question and renew itself, otherwise, as Ionesco taught us in *La Leçon*, learning can become fatal to the learner.

Testimonial 5
Karin A. Grimnes
Department of Biology
Alma College
Alma, Michigan 48801

(1) Although I have had no formal training in acting techniques, I have become increasingly aware of their importance to the quality and effectiveness of my teaching. As my teaching style has evolved, I have paid special attention to the use of my body and the use of space in the classroom. I am not afraid to use these techniques in a humorous or self-deprecating mode if needed. My primary goal is to increase student motivation, learning, and attentiveness in any way that works.

(2) In the classroom, I am in continual motion. I frequently find myself pacing while I talk, and often gesture toward the board for emphasis. I write notes in outline form, and write very fast. Consequently, I spend little time with my back to the class. Instead, I usually say things in more than one way and rely on extensive use of analogies to get my points across. I enjoy sweeping gestures and dramatic pauses. Sometimes I cheer for correct answers or make victory gestures. I maintain eye contact with most members of the class, and therefore I can often tell when a point is not understood.

(3) I teach courses in biology, and one (developmental biology) involves an appreciation of three-dimensional structures in development. I describe

the events of development using myself as the embryo, twisting and turning my upper body as needed. Then I am able to ask students which side of the embryo is on the yolk and other questions about the relationship of embryonic parts. I encourage them to do the same motions and will often grab a student and make them bend, and then describe the events going on around them. I warn them at the beginning of the term that I may get physical with them. As I am a short person, this statement amuses them, and they usually allow me this privilege.

(4) Another helpful technique to illustrate moving layers involves putting on two jackets and demonstrating how some layers must fuse before others. By asking them to explain what I have done, I can quickly determine their level of understanding. I may ask them to repeat the demonstration. Most of these techniques I use in the lab where I might be talking with three students at a time since I do not wish to embarrass students by forcing them to act the motions out in front of the entire class.

(5) Another class I teach is invertebrate biology. I illustrate crab foraging behavior, spider orientation, and scorpion attacks by waving arms and leaping or lunging. I may ask students to demonstrate prey escape behavior while I play predator. I have found that the behavior demonstrations help solidify concepts and create an "episode" that is remembered intact for a long period of time. Of course, most of these demonstrations are accompanied by appropriate hissing and sucking noises.

(6) When I have a major point to emphasize, or I can tell that student interest is flagging, I invade their space. I may lean on the first tier of desks in the raked lecture hall, or ask the students to make fists so I can use them for a demonstration. Students are immediately more attentive when their space is compromised, but I try not to overuse this technique. When I am presenting an argument, I may present one side at one end of the classroom and the other view some distance away. I then ask questions and run to the side which the answers support. When I bring up contradictory information, it may be accompanied by a melodramatic gesture of despair.

(7) I believe in the skills I have listed above; these skills have been added slowly to my repertoire. I am always searching for new ideas, but have discovered that not all techniques are suitable for my teaching style. I can usually identify inappropriate techniques, but if I have any doubt I use a few students as victims. They let me know when I am off base.

Testimonial 6
Roger A. Hall
Department of Theater and Dance
James Madison University
Harrisonburg, Virginia 22807

(1) One of the courses I teach to my undergraduates is playwriting, and I am struck by the ways in which constructing a lecture or a classroom exercise is similar to writing a scene or a short play. Plays are but human will striving to attain goals and confronted by opposition and obstacles. Teachers can use that same scheme to present information that induces questions and creates suspense.

(2) One of the lessons that playwriting has taught me is to pose questions for the characters and for the audience in the very first lines of a play. The same is true for a class, where the audience is the students. A teacher needs to structure material in order to pose questions at the start of a class. When I'm talking about tragedy, I'll ask, "Why for 2,500 years have audiences gone to see plays about awful things happening to decent people?" But the questions don't have to be direct. If I hang up five different kinds of masks before the class begins, the questions about what those different faces represent, how they might have been used, and how I intend to use them in the class are inherent in the props before I've said a word. Asking questions and getting the "audience" to formulate questions leads to problem-solving, and problem solving leads to critical thinking.

(3) Conflict is another lesson of playwriting applicable to teaching. We teachers forget sometimes that the factual information and the standard opinions we impart were not always so concrete. Evolution, the shape of the earth, and the center of the solar system once sparked dangerous clashes of opinion. Experts regarded the plate theory of continental drift as simplistic and laughable until just twenty-five or thirty years ago. History, science, even art and culture are rife with conflict and obstacles. Civilizations, after all, do not simply progress. They face obstacles such as food shortages or pollution, and they struggle to overcome them. Conflicts not only make subject matter exciting, but also reveal to students the human character of the material. I encourage teachers to see learning as a series of conflicts and obstacles rather than an inevitable narrative of "this and then this and then this."

(4) Another lesson common to playwriting and to other forms of writing is to write about what you know best. Similarly, teachers should use what they know best. I still recall the stories of my eighth grade American history teacher. He made us feel the sensations of a war by telling us about his experiences in World War II. He made the battle of Gettysburg come alive by describing the terrain he'd walked himself. All of us, no matter how

mundane our lives, have personal memories and experiences to draw upon, and whatever personal references we can use to connect solidly to the material will linger in our students' minds.

(5) "Climax" is another playwriting element that can help teachers structure a good class. Whether I'm working with playwrights or performers, I'll always ask, "What's the climax of this scene or play?" Teachers should ask themselves the same question. Students won't remember everything, so a good teacher must determine the most important part. If a student will only remember one thing from today's class or lecture, what should it be? Then build to that. Emphasize that. Make it the climax of the class.

(6) The use of these playwriting techniques — inducing questions, identifying conflicts and obstacles, using personal connections to material, and developing material to a climax — will help a teacher create classes with drama: classes that generate interest, sustain suspense, and leave students with a feeling that something important has been achieved.

Testimonial 7
Carol L. Harrison
Department of Humanities
Medaille College
Buffalo, New York 14214

(1) After using acting skills and techniques in the classroom in varied courses over the span of twenty years, I can readily attest to their aid in maintaining both the vibrancy and quality of learning taking place. So often, professors looking for ways to improve upon the traditional pedagogy of lecture-discussion overlook the simple and simply fun aspect of incorporating acting and simulation principles into teaching.

(2) I have often heard from beleaguered, burned-out colleagues, "I can't act" or "You can't be sure students are learning anything" to "It's a waste of good time better spent." Not so. For classroom freshness, student vitality, and assessable student learning outcomes, nothing beats enhancing a lecture or reiterating a difficult theoretical concept like acting. Yes, admittedly acting does demand a lot of the professor in terms of preparation time, thorough coverage of the concept to be learned, and student involvement. But in the long run, the learning that takes place and the enjoyment of learning are worth the extra effort.

(3) Whether it is a literature or writing class, I always follow three cardinal rules of acting in the class. First, keep the activity relevant to the concept to be learned. For example, in a simulation technique I use in an argumentation and persuasion writing class geared to pre-law majors, one

day I bring to class with me, beside the usual old briefcase, my coat and purse. I intentionally leave the lecture hall door open. No one seems to notice these slight changes. I begin the lecture as usual on the topic of observation, detail, and description. After a few minutes and with my back to the class, I write the class objectives for the day on the board. At a pre-arranged verbal signal, a student from another class runs into the lecture hall and furtively snatches my purse left purposely on the front desk.

(4) The class objective is now open for discussion. As in the real world, I ask the class to give an accurate description of the thief in every detail — the same question witnesses are asked to answer after a surprise event. Of course, no one gives an accurate description, which opens up the relevant but tangential topic of adjectives and accuracy. How tall is tall? Exactly what color of blue? I then request the "thief" to return so that the class may have a good look. More discussion ensues and leads to the next class topic of sequencing of events and types of order in critical thinking and writing.

(5) The second rule is to use props. As in the previously cited example, the purse and coat were considered props. Props enhance the "reality" of acting. They make the involvement of the imagination immediate and visual. Props may be complex or simple. I try to keep the props simple mainly because it takes up less class preparation time and less set up time. It also permits handling of simple props by students when called for and allows more class time for discussion.

(6) A doctor's bag, a feather boa, and a briefcase and newspaper serve as simple props in a basic college-level writing course discussing the importance of active voice with verbs. Pre-chosen student volunteers from the class are picked to demonstrate the variety of ways to dress up the rather simple verb "to walk." Our first example is the harassed businessman late for an important appointment. The student picks up the briefcase and the newspaper and in front of the class (space has been blocked out for this activity before class begins) shows how Mr. X would walk to his appointment. Surprise! "To walk" now becomes "walked briskly," "hurried," "scurried," and "raced."

(7) Dr. Y on call with his doctor's bag now demonstrates "marching." "Walking proudly" down the hospital corridors. Finally, Miss Z with her feather boa elicits a different kind of walk. "To walk" now becomes "strutting," "sauntering," "sashshaying" down the street. What we find in terms of learning outcomes is that students in this class indeed know the other terms for the simple word walk, but never used them. Our little acting activity accompanied by the use of simple props set fire to vocabulary building and encouraged the usage of other less familiar words. The lesson ends with an introduction to Roget's *Thesaurus* and a class eager and willing to try new words in writing.

(8) The third cardinal principle in use of acting activities is perhaps the most obvious—involve the students. It is often the temptation of a professor who is a natural "ham" to hog the stage. Let the students become the principals, for active involvement encourages active learning and successful retention.

(9) In the freshman writing course, teaching the basic rhetorical modes can be anything but exciting. They are standard and unvaried; however, through acting even the most static mode can become an exciting and valuable exercise. Take, for example, cause and effect. I always leave cause and effect last, not because it is the most difficult, but because for my science and social science majors it is the most demonstrable.

(10) In this exercise, I come to class five minutes late. I am dressed in the costume of a fashionable young woman. My class has been told that they are counselors who must get to the root or cause of this young woman's problem by the end of the period. They may, in turn, ask her any questions they like. As the "patient," I will exhibit all of the "effects" of her illness or problem. During the course of the period, I take out of my purse the picture of a young man and sigh. I chew gum; I act distracted. I act morose and depressed. I cough and cry into my Kleenex. I answer questions laconically. Gradually, they build up a list of "effects" from which they can deduce a probable "cause"—she's heartbroken because she's been jilted! On an examination, they surely remember cause and effect!

(11) Thus any instructor with a little imagination and initiative can become an actor in the classroom. It is not only challenging, but it provides the life and vitality—the spark—to the traditional pedagogy of lecture discussion. However, a word of caution: acting and simulation activities are not a replacement or coverup for inadequacy of content or preparation. Students are quick to spot a quack. Following the cardinal rules of relevancy to topical content, use of simple props, and student involvement will guarantee a successful acting activity and student learning outcomes, no matter what the subject matter. Shakespeare needn't be dull nor lessons in history or psychology boring—add some acting activity, no matter how small, to your class and see for yourself. It's good pedagogical fun!

Testimonial 8
Bebe Lavin and Jerry M. Lewis
Department of Sociology
Kent State University
Kent, Ohio 44242

(1) This is a dialogue on the relationship between performance and teaching between Professors Bebe Lavin and Jerry M. Lewis. Their focus in

this dialogue is on the very large "Introduction to Sociology" class that they both teach. This class with enrollments of nearly seven hundred students meets in the university auditorium.

(2) Dr. Bebe Lavin (BL): Over the years you and I have spent a lot of hours talking about the importance of teaching and ways to improve what we do. The large section is a real challenge to us, and what I've realized is how differently we approach that teaching.

(3) Dr. Jerry M. Lewis (JML): That's true, and we clearly have different views on the place of performance in our lecturing.

(4) BL: The fact that this is a mass class taught in a unique setting of an auditorium demands of faculty considerable imagination as to teaching methods and style.

(5) JML: That the course is taught in an auditorium contributes to its theatrical aspects for me. I walk in the side door of the auditorium, and it is actually like going into the New York or Chicago legitimate stage theater. There is even murmuring among the audience.

(6) BL: It's interesting that the theater is your image, the gestalt you have when you come to class. It is not that for me.

(7) JML: Putting on the floating mike also creates a theatrical feeling for me as well. Sometimes I feel like I am getting ready to do a one-person show.

(8) BL: So for you each class requires a performance, and it does for me too. But the symbolism of the theater is more integral to your teaching than it is for mine.

(9) JML: Right. And there are three ways I perform that are important to my teaching. First, I tell jokes. The jokes are stories and are related to the material of the lecture. For example, to illustrate the concept of "the definition of the situation" or differential perceptions, I tell the story of Matilda, an eighty-five-year-old woman who goes to her physician who, after an examination, informs her that she is pregnant. "But, Doctor, I'm eighty-five years old." The doctor says, "I know, but you're pregnant." She decides to call her husband, Fred, who is eighty-nine years old. He picks up the phone, to hear Matilda say excitedly, "Fred, I'm pregnant." He says, "Who is this?"

(10) I must admit that I enjoy the fact that I have made over six hundred people laugh. I also worry that too much humor gets in the way of the lecture. Do you tell jokes?

(11) BL: Rarely. For me telling a joke requires too much risk-taking. To do so I feel I must rehearse, and the recital seems stilted and awkward. But I do think humor is an important tool. I look for the ironic or droll in a situation to make an idea understandable. It surprises me how often it is possible to inject a humorous note in a lecture, but it is most often spontaneous, unplanned. We are both recognizing that humor is a

necessary tool for the lecture process. What other tools are important to your performance?

(12) JML: I do short imaginary dialogues with fictional characters. One of them is "Martha," my wife; another is "a student from Ashtabula," who is naive, [Ashtabula is a small town in northeast Ohio]; and third is a bright student who knows the answer to a question I have posed.

(13) BL: Tell me more.

(14) JML: I use the skit between me and my characters to make a point for the class, and for me that performance has more impact than the usual lecture. For example, Martha is with me when I talk about private and public space. I make a comment on it, noting a performance that a young couple is putting on. For example, I will say, "See that couple over by the Coke machine—they are fighting but they don't want others to know." Martha: "How do you know?" JML: "Because . . . and then I explain to Martha the sociological ideas involved. Martha will also chastise me if she thinks the joke I told is off-color.

(15) BL: So the fictional characters have a personality of their own that students can identify with over the semester. They're like Edgar Bergen's Charlie or Mortimer. And they have a role in your performance. I like that. Now, what is the third way that you use the theatrical motif in your teaching?

(16) JML: I play games with students. For example, when I teach Eric Erikson's eight stages of socialization, I play a game of softball catch with students in the class. So during class I will play roles from an infant to an elderly person playing catch. The students do seem to remember Erikson's stages.

(17) BL: You're really "physical" in your performance, aren't you? Moving about, up and down aisles, playing ball with students. Although I do move about, my range is much more limited than what you're suggesting. I am just not comfortable playing that vigorous a role. Is there any worry that students will not take you seriously with all these games and other role plays?

(18) JML: I think the students appreciate the humor. My qualitative course evaluations show this. What does worry me is that my colleagues both in and out of sociology will judge my teaching as frivolous.

(19) BL: I would think that the important point is whether the "acts" that you use are effective in teaching the ideas you want students to learn. There is no question in my mind that we both focus on that as the primary issue. But you incorporate techniques in your teaching that are much more akin to theater and entertainment than I do, and I have little doubt that this makes your class lively and interesting.

(20) JML: Don't you think you are performing when you lecture?

(21) BL: Definitely. I am concerned about setting a scene, establishing

my persona or character part from that first lecture on and sustaining it so students know what to expect. The part I want to play is someone whom the students are convinced is qualified to teach the course, believes in the importance of the subject matter, and is concerned about them as students.

(22) JML: But that sounds so stuffy. What do you do so that the class is not boring?

(23) BL: Well, I do use humor, as I said before. And perhaps even more than you, I do involve the audience. For example, I use games, but differently than you. I set up scenarios or "what if" situations a lot, and ask students to give me their responses. You know, the typical one is the family of a father, his wife, his son, and his mother out in a boat that capsizes. He can save two people. Amazingly, when asked whom they'd save, students will arrive at quite different conclusions, giving me a great opportunity to discuss cultural values and differences. As much as possible I use ways to involve students, and even in our large class, it is remarkable how much students will respond and get involved. I guess I don't set the scene as much as I have a developing script. Sometimes we get off track, but most of the time students make the point of the lecture, and in their own words and understanding. I think this is valuable.

(24) JML: No question about that. What intrigues me is that we both get nearly the same ratings from our students and peers as to the effectiveness of the teaching and the teacher, but we are different in our approach right down to the way we think of the setting.

(25) BL: Frankly, we both are effective, but I suspect that your class is more fun because of your use of the theatrical. At the same time I realize that there are some actions with which I am not comfortable. The question seems to be the extent to which techniques are transferable. Some "acts" can be taught and used; others, it seems to me, are easy because they are a part of one's makeup, yet quite foreign to someone else. I might be able to play Juliet, but not Desdemona.

Testimonial 9
Douglas Light
Department of Biology
Ripon College
Ripon, Wisconsin 54971

(1) The lights dim. The curtain rises. A man appears on the screen; he is reading a letter. The camera closes in on his face, and a tear can be seen emerging from his right eye. Soon there are tears streaming from both eyes. His expression of sadness is filled with such torment the audience begins to cry. Although the audience is cognizant that they are watching a celluloid

fantasy, they still cry. Why? Good acting sweeps people away and involves them in the mood of the acting production. It is the ability to involve an audience that a teacher must master if he/she is to be completely successful at teaching.

(2) The best way I know to involve students and persuade them to learn is to show unbridled enthusiasm. I express enthusiasm through excitement and animation of my voice, hands, face, and body, and by my words. I lecture with the exuberance of a football announcer describing a 96-yard touchdown run. The response from students to this enthusiasm has been very rewarding. For example, one student wrote on a course evaluation, "How can the professor get so enthusiastic about osmosis? His enthusiasm did convince me that there must be something interesting about it, so I listened and learned." Another student commented, "How can the professor be so energetic at 8:00 AM; it's absolutely revolting, however, it does keep me interested." A third student stated, "I don't understand how the professor can maintain his level of enthusiasm. I'm glad he does because it gets me through the lecture." I cannot overemphasize the importance of enthusiasm to involve students.

(3) Although essential, I have found that enthusiasm alone is not sufficient to be a good teacher. The difference between a good actor and a great one is that the latter not only memorizes the script but also "becomes" the character portrayed by knowing all there is to know about that character. By analogy, it is absolutely essential that a teacher be completely (within reason) knowledgeable about his/her subject matter. This does not mean just memorizing the lecture material but also being familiar with pertinent background information. To help keep command of the subjects I teach, I read all assignments in the textbooks and pertinent journals and books on a regular basis. I also prepare questions to ask students before class starts. This permits me to present the subject in a more relaxed, flowing manner and to make it more meaningful to students by providing interesting examples and connections. In addition, it allows me to answer a greater number of questions from students as well as providing better explanations. A teacher that cannot answer a sufficient number of questions from students is tantamount to an actor forgetting the script; very quickly the audience becomes disinterested. A good command of the subject also permits me to include suspense and surprise in my teaching. For example, I will often pose a series of questions at the beginning of class and answer them during the lecture. Like an old "cliff-hanger," I will leave some questions unanswered until the next class meeting. I believe this helps foster critical thinking. Rewards for long hours of preparation are plentiful. Student evaluations have commented that a knowledgeable teacher is much more interesting than one appearing to grope for answers, and that trying to solve questions is more challenging, and therefore more fun than a lecture.

(4) For an actor, control of voice expression is important for indicating emotion; for a teacher it is used for emphasis. I stress important points by speaking loudly and in an animated manner, whereas tangential points are presented in a more relaxed manner. I have found that my change in voice intensity and expression has helped students distinguish more easily between important points and ancillary ones. Further, I have found that addition of humor helps break the intensity of a lecture and recharge the students' energy level.

(5) In conclusion, I incorporate enthusiasm, animation, suspense, surprise, voice control, and humor in my lectures. Further, I work hard at being knowledgeable about the subjects I teach. Because all of this requires a tremendous expenditure of energy, an immediate litmus test for my success is leaving a classroom or laboratory feeling physically and emotionally drained.

Testimonial 10
Anthony J. Lisska
Department of Philosophy
Denison University
Granville, Ohio 43023

(1) I have found that using humor at an appropriate time in a class is an effective way both to make a point and to keep student interest alive. Of course, humor cannot take the place of instruction, but it can help to develop the instructional process. Every instructor has a captive audience, and there are certain ways to move an audience that are more effective than others. When I taught the Philosophy of Education, I customarily sent my students to the theater department to enroll in acting classes. The students considering secondary school teaching needed to become very outgoing and spontaneous in their delivery. While instruction is never coextensive with entertainment, nonetheless to learn how to work an audience should not be downplayed.

(2) One example of humor in teaching philosophy comes from a consideration of Aristotelian ethics. In his *Nicomachean Ethics*, Aristotle goes to great lengths to indicate that specific circumstances and the particular situation are extremely important in determining the correctness of a moral judgment. Hence the particular context of a situation is morally relevant in determining the moral appropriateness of an action.

(3) The example I use is both humorous and experiential. I build the scene from my experience as a freshly minted sixteen-year-old driver. The scene goes like this: My two brothers and I had the family car out for a spin. I am the oldest, and I was introducing my brothers into the thrills of 1950s drag

racing. We took our parents' car (a 1953 Chrysler with fluid drive—that means you had a clutch with an automatic shift). One can embellish the story by thinking of "Happy Days" or "Grease." I tell the students that my brothers and I got the car out on a country road about 9:00 o'clock on a cool summer night. We decided to see what it would do as a potential dragster. I put the car in low gear, floored the accelerator as much as I could with the clutch in. The engine revved up, then I popped that clutch to see if this Chrysler sedan would accelerate quickly enough to be a potentially fine dragster. As soon as I popped the clutch, all we could hear was "crash, bang, ping, ping, ping, thump," and then the car would not go forward. [Slight pause]—and then I mention "Of course, I tore the transmission out of the car!"

(4) Here we were, my brothers and I, stranded on a country road. My younger brother kept telling me I had really made a mess and our father was going to have me drawn and quartered and then tarred and feathered. I got home paralyzed with fear. I was a psychic mess with fear overriding everything. I thought my father would certainly banish me from the family after taking me to the woodshed. I climbed the stairs to our apartment, shaking, knees quivering, heart fluttering. I had just torn the transmission out of the family car—I didn't use my own car for that, but the family car! He certainly would have the justification to punish me with gusto.

(5) I found my father and told him what I had done. I was expecting to get cracked across the face with the back of his hand. My dad looked at me, straight in the eyes, and said slowly and earnestly, "Son, you can't treat a car that way!"

(6) That statement of my father's, I tell my students, had more of a profound effect on me than had he punished me with an old-fashioned whipping and grounded me for six months.

(7) Of course, the Chrysler was fixed. The mechanic gave my father the two gears which I had stripped—one was chrome with no teeth left at all, and the other was gray metal with half of the teeth gone. Well past my graduate school days, I kept those gears on my desk as a reminder *not* to do stupid things.

(8) I tell my students that this was an example of a person seizing upon a particular situation and acting in a certain way which had a profound effect. In addition to Aristotelian overtones, this example has an existential dimension to it by indicating the importance of the particular situation. The buildup of the story is humorous—the students laugh and they can relate to it. And then they do see the final punch line concerning a wise father who knew how to react to a prodigal son.

Testimonial 11
William M. Mahoney
Department of History
West Virginia Wesleyan College
Buckhannon, West Virginia 26201

(1) As a history professor at a small liberal arts college, I have spent a decade learning my craft in an environment conducive to the development of educational acting skills and the awareness of the classroom as a stage upon which the instructor may combine aspects of the lecturer and the performer.   Crucial to my own approach to teaching has been the establishment of a comfortable relationship with students in reasonably sized classes, ranging from Western Civilization and Humanities surveys to upper-level courses in European history.

(2) In my view, the important first step in creating a comfortable classroom environment is a process of self-disclosure, whereby the instructor breaks down some of the more formalized elements of the teacher-student relationship in favor of a more personalized approach. From the instructor's standpoint, this means knowing students' names and engaging them in conversation before and after class as a means of converting strangers into a receptive audience.   In addition, it is helpful if the students view the instructor as a real person with a personality and interests that extend beyond the boundaries of the classroom and the course. The key to all of this is accessibility, and it has been especially important for me to develop a less formal relationship with students so that I am more comfortable in "performing" as a lecturer and discussion leader. The more comfortable I am with a class, the more spontaneous and creative I try to become in explaining history to majors and non-majors alike.

(3) Personally, a successful process of self-disclosure affects my actual teaching in two distinct ways. First of all, it allows me to overcome my own reticence about addressing an audience and therefore to utilize humor, personal touches, and even performance techniques in attempting to make history more than just a collection of names and dates. Second, the creation of a comfortable classroom environment allows me to abandon class notes in favor of greater use of physical space and a more spontaneous and impressionistic style of lecturing.   The notes remain available for consultation during a lecture, but freedom of movement and the element of spontaneity take the instructor a step closer to utilizing acting skills without sacrificing narrative continuity or depth of detail in a lecture.

(4) When discussing the performance aspects of lecturing, one can mean a number of things, from knowing one's lines to utilizing movement and gestures to draw a student's attention to the story lurking behind the facts. Given the wealth of dramatic events and fascinating individuals in history,

the study of the past lends itself to storytelling techniques and to role-playing on the part of both teacher and student. In addition to using novels and plays as auxiliary readings in some courses, I often rely on storytelling techniques in an attempt to bring characters and events to life or to recreate a setting or environment to help students visualize the material. For instance, relating an "eyewitness" account of life in the trenches during the First World War or the fall of the Bastille during the French Revolution can create a storyline and characters for historical facts found in the textbook.

(5) Finally, a degree of role-playing can also enhance the performance aspects of classroom teaching by personalizing the material from the perspective of a recognizable individual. By having Louis XIV describe his own achievements or Hitler and Mussolini explain why the voters must choose between them or chaos, the instructor can personalize history by luring students out of their own perspectives and presenting historical events at the level of individual experience. Perhaps the most effective attempt at role-playing involved my taking on the persona of a German terrorist of the Baader-Meinhof variety who was a guest on a popular American talk show. With the students serving as the studio audience, they became so caught up in debating and denouncing the terrorist that classroom realities disappeared, and I sat playing a smug, bourgeois terrorist engaged in less-than-cordial conversation with a fairly hostile, yet well-behaved, crowd. Unfortunately, I was eventually forced to remind the class that my name was not "Klaus" and that there were a few other historical matters to attend to in the time remaining. However, although reality had returned, the brief exchange in role-playing mode had raised issues and introduced perspectives that could not be found in normal textbook or lecture formats.

Testimonial 12
Daniel J. McBrayer
Department of Education and Psychology
Berry College
Mount Berry, Georgia 30149-5019

(1) As a teacher of psychology I find that my subject matter is quite easy to apply to "everyday" situations in the lives of undergraduate students. This process involves actively demonstrating the concept being taught, much like the actress would demonstrate the feelings and nuances in her role on stage. This demonstration allows the student to operationalize the concept in his mind and transfer its application to multiple situations in his life. This demonstration is accomplished through acting out, sometimes in role-play, the concept in ways that are personal, dramatic, and/or humorous.

(2) Just as an actress in an intimate theater (I teach classes of 20–35) will move close to her audience to grab their attention, a teacher can use proxemics to drive home a point. I spend considerable time "in the audience." I always have two to five empty chairs around the room and use these chairs to sit next to a student I am questioning or challenging. When seated I am at eye level and engage in a conversation, while the other students witness—sometimes in awe! At times I will role-play with the student, and at other times I will role-play with an imaginary student in my empty chair. The power of this strategy is remembered and discussed among the students for weeks and months. Using movement, proximity, and demonstration in class can actually be more powerful than acting on stage because of the interaction it affords.

(3) There are times when I create a preplanned, written scenario to be acted out with preselected students. This modification of a script gets the students directly involved in the teaching of the concept. At other times I have a colleague in my department enter my classroom at a prearranged time to share news, attack, embrace, and so on. This strategy will "bring to life" a concept we are discussing (e.g., eyewitness testimony, perception, emotion). In each case, we (as actors) are using voice, emotion, proximity, and reality as teaching techniques.

(4) As a method of creating suspense in the audience, I frequently use two strategies. Undergraduate students are often quite gullible. Using this to enhance learning, and awareness, can be very insightful for them. A strategy that works at my institution is to share with them some developing administrative thought or policy that will impact their lives. These situations are, in the end, clearly communicated as fictitious. However, while I am sharing the potential policy with them, it is very real. Numerous concepts from a psychology textbook can be tied to the thinking and behavior of administrators. Students learn the concepts and also get a chance to think and respond to the administrative behavior. This process involves them, forces them to see alternatives to their thinking, and causes them to crystalize their thoughts on the topic. In a sense this is manipulating an audience as we would in acting—yet not in a pejorative manner.

(5) The second strategy to create interest and suspense in the audience is the use of my imaginary family. We have unusual names like Vachael, Oral, Alred, Orval, Bertha, Bobby Jack, and so on. We also have unusual occupations and live in cities with very unique names. This uses humor and serves in being "catchy." Students will notice how Vachael seems to be living, using, or misunderstanding the concept being taught, but may not pay as much attention if it was my sister Allison.

(6) The above techniques clearly involve acting in teaching. Every good teacher does not need to use strategies such as these to be effective. I use them because I enjoy going to class and choose to make the learning

environment fit my personality style – and that is to enjoy the subject matter, make it come alive, and make it last beyond the next test! My acting experience, outside the classroom, has been somewhat limited. I have learned how to act, and how to teach, on the same stage! I believe, given the experience base of the current undergraduate student population, we need to meet them part way – which suggests that they have been accustomed to being "entertained." These strategies do not "limit" my responsibility to teach content; they simply enhance the content, and make it a part of the student's reality.

Testimonial 13
Scott Richardson
Department of Modern and Classical Languages
St. John's University
Collegeville, Minnesota 56321

(1) As a classics professor I regularly feel on the defensive in non-major courses. The value inherent in the study of Greek literature and culture is to me self-evident, but not so to a good portion of our students nowadays. To those oriented toward practicality and "relevance" (a word generally used with a baiting tone in my presence), I must make a special effort to earn their interest by showing that works written in a dead language by people who lived before 1960 actually do have a strong bearing on their own lives and world. Besides directly addressing this issue as we approach the texts, I very often make use of a couple routines.

(2) Every college student in the country watches the David Letterman show. Once a week he starts the program with the Viewer Mail segment, which involves facetious replies to usually facetious letters, a parody of the "Sixty Minutes" bit. Toward the end of every semester in all of my courses, including language courses, I start the class with my own Viewer Mail. I write the letters myself, of course, and prepare the replies, which I deliver from memory as though talking to a TV audience. Some of the letters have to do with the worth of studying dead languages or the literature and culture of dead civilizations; some deal with the worth of education in general; some poke fun at my own interests or pedagogical habits. I try to make most of the letters sound almost (but not quite) like letters that people would write who had no understanding of what a liberal arts education entails or why I am teaching what and how I do. My implicit mockery of those who would think this way brings out in the open some of the doubts actually felt by many and at the same time makes the students feel superior to the morons who would so bluntly call attention to their own philistinism. I pretend to take the letters seriously and to give an off-the-wall reply that

tacitly (but clearly) hints at the true value of a classical education. This routine is always well received and involves spontaneous group participation stemming from everyone's acquaintance with the TV show. The surprise factor is important, I think, so I would recommend it as a one-shot gimmick. It works best with more than half of the term over, since it depends on the students' familiarity with the subject matter and with the professor's attitude toward the field.

(3) Greek tragedy and mythology, foreign as they seem, have a great deal of "relevance" to everyone's life, and a classics professor would have little trouble luring the students to see their own lives and societies in light of the grand stories and dramas of the Greeks. My favorite routine comes with the discussion of the god Dionysus, which I usually center around Euripides' *The Bacchae*, his play about Dionysus' revenge on his blasphemous relatives. Dionysus is the god of the irrational element of the universe and in human nature, a force we neglect or repress at our peril, yet to follow it blindly leads to catastrophe. How to handle the Dionysian vis-à-vis the Apollonian in ourselves is one of our biggest struggles; how should we respect Dionysus' power yet not become devotees? To bring this character to life, I invoke the cult film *The Rocky Horror Picture Show*, whose main character is a stunning avatar of Dionysus: he is effeminate and virile, gentle and vicious, hedonistic and vengeful, soft and powerful; his philosophical tenet is "give yourself over to absolute pleasure," and he is unmerciful toward anyone who stands in his way. He introduces himself with a rousing rock 'n' roll song, "Sweet Transvestite," whose tune I have stolen for my own song, following closely the original lyrics, about Dionysus, in which I present the central features of the god's character, the main plot elements of the play, and several of the technical terms of Bacchic worship. I pass around the lyrics, get out my guitar, make sure they are familiar with the film song (either tape, videotape, or my own performance), and then lead them all through this Dionysian hymn. Everyone — even those who are shy — joins in uninhibited. They come away with a vivid picture of this bit of Greek culture.

Testimonial 14
Martha Rogers
Department of Telecommunications
Bowling Green State University
Bowling Green, Ohio 43402

(1) It's my belief that good teaching is 25 percent education and 75 percent inspiration. The most valuable lesson a student can learn in the classroom is that the subject is fascinating, exploring it is meaningful and

worthwhile, and learning is fun. Students who are thus motivated will take the tools I provide and *teach themselves* – by careful reading of text, by attendance (physical and mental) to lecture material, to be sure. But students who are truly *inspired* will explore additional materials in the library, will seek discussion on the topic outside the classroom, will explore the chance for application and for articulation of their ideas.

(2) To me, the best way to generate excitement in students is to generate it myself. Good actors who receive positive reviews are often described as exhibiting a high energy level. That energy is contagious. Of course, my job is to walk into the classroom well prepared with my material thorough, refreshed and updated, and well organized. That's the 25 percent education part. But the real challenge is to teach that material each time as if it's the first time. Every "performance" must retain the excitement of opening night. For every member of the audience, after all, it is just that.

(3) Every professor has her or his own style. What seems to work for me includes lots of eye contact, voice modulation, and poignant pauses. (I sometimes hear a southern Baptist preacher in the room and realize it's only myself.) But however dramatic the hand gestures or however careful and clear the diction (I'm trying to improve this), the one most important element to me, the one that cannot be faked, is enthusiasm – sheer, delighted *exuberance* with the topic and the audience. I hope to give the impression that I can't wait to hear what I'm going to say next. If my goal is to educate my students a little and inspire them a lot, it's as important that I raise my eyebrows as much as review questions, that I pace the classroom as well as the material, that I look over the rim of my eyeglasses as carefully as I look over student term papers.

(4) The effect is everything. Whatever my students may think of *me* when they leave the classroom (impossible, stuck up, professional or not, smart or know-it-all) doesn't matter. What *does* matter is what they think of *themselves*. If they are challenged to do the job better, to learn more, to know more, do more, be more, I can see it in their eyes. It's worth it to wave my arms, pound a desk, shout, use funny voices – whatever it takes to get a point across and watch for laughing, for looks of concern, for incredulity, for thoughtfulness, and ultimately for the look that says "I've never thought of that before!"

Testimonial 15
Charlotte Rotkin
Professor of English
Pace University
Pelham Manor, New York 10803

(1) I teach literature to a diverse population of undergraduates at a large urban university in New York, and have found that the thespian's technique lends itself to success in the classroom. I use theatrics as an efficient and pedagogically sound method of presenting information in an entertaining manner. A dramatic delivery and self-deprecating irony can be extremely effective in engaging students' attention. When I rely on humor as a teaching tool, I notice that some of the usual antipathy to literature is allayed. I therefore open every semester with the following remarks: "I know you didn't register for this course because you love English! You're here because it's required. So try to make the best of it. Pretend you've turned on your television set and the channel selector got stuck on me!"

(2) Responsive smiles and the relaxation of body postures result in a change in the electrical charge in the room. From a negative atmosphere of uncertainty, animosity, and fear, the electrical current has become, to some extent, a positive one. I've captured some members of the audience. But I'll be on stage another forty minutes and I can't afford to lose them. So I present my regulations regarding decorum in an institution of higher learning. I say, in a semi-authoritarian tone, "I have two rules in this class. There will be no hitting and no vulgarity!" The ensuing explosion of laughter is occasionally interspersed with the query, "What's vulgarity?"

(3) In addition to being exposed to the literary element of irony, by the time the first session is over, the class will have touched upon vocabulary enhancement via the definitions of irony, tone, and vulgarity. They will have been apprised of appropriate classroom behavior for college students, and they will have become aware of my demand for their active participation in the learning process, all painlessly presented through wit.

(4) Our shared laughter creates a temporary bond between us. In order not to lose that precarious sense of identification between the student-audience and me, I, as instructor-performer, try to bring into being a theatrical use of available space, and I do that by envisioning the area separating my lectern from the first row of seats as the imagined apron of a stage. The space separating audience and performer can be bridged by stepping in front of the lectern and inclining the upper portion of the body over the imagined apron in responsive attention to a student's question or comment. Since my teaching strategy makes fundamental use of the Socratic method, I begin to present probing questions on the art of evaluating literature and the skills needed for successful communication. And when I

offer students the choice of responding to my questions verbally or in essay form, a lively discussion ensues.

(5) Most students are receptive to and gratified by the personal attention and eye contact I make as I move through the class-audience and attend (like a talkshow host) to the student whose hand is raised. When a point of view which I may not have considered is brought forth, I pause and indicate by my ruminating manner that I hadn't thought of that. I then take time to absorb it out loud, with an occasional assist from the originator of the idea, or from a similarly inclined other student. When I reach the perspective from which the students are coming, I generally nod in agreement and bowing slightly will say, "That's a very valid point you've got there. If I were wearing a hat, I'd take it off to you." Periodically a cap is proffered, and my gesture of a sweeping bow is well received. Although some students have difficulty analyzing irony, most recognize its intended wit in word, tone, or gesture and are responsive to its gentle humor.

Testimonial 16
Arno Selco
Department of Theater Arts
Ithaca College
Ithaca, New York 14850

(1) I teach acting technique in a BFA acting program. What I teach my students might be used by teachers of many subjects to improve their teaching.

(2) There are four rudiments of acting technique: (1) the objective; (2) the obstacle; (3) the stake; and (4) the tactics. The objective is what the actor decides his character wants essentially, the character's primary desire, goal, purpose, or intention. The obstacle is what the actor decides his character basically must leap over, remove, or negotiate to achieve the objective. The stake is what the actor decides his character will lose if the objective is not achieved. The tactics are the means by which he decides his character pursues the objective.

(3) To illustrate: if an actor were cast in Tennessee Williams' *A Streetcar Named Desire* as Blanche DuBois, she might decide that Blanche's objective is to find a sanctuary from the nightmarish existence she has led by convincing her sister Stella to take her into her home. The obstacle to her achieving her objective could be Stella's husband, Stanley Kowalski; Stanley opposes Blanche because her pursuit invades his privacy. But Blanche persists, because her stake in living with Stella is as high as possible: without Stella's protection, Blanche is too frail in body and mind to survive. The actor playing Blanche could choose as her character's tactics to flatter Stella, to threaten her, to befriend her, to warn her, to inspire her, and so on.

(4) The very same rudiments that enable an actor to create his or her character may be used to teach most any subject effectively. First, the teacher determines his/her objective. This may prove to be more difficult than it sounds. A teacher is likely to encounter the same difficulty in choosing an objective as does an actor: the crux of the decision is to choose the best objective out of the many that inevitably pop into one's mind. As I repeat to my acting students, "When it comes to your objective, only one to a customer." Every teacher will find it clarifying, liberating, and empowering to determine which essential aspect of his subject he desires or intends to impart to his students through a particular lesson, lecture, lab, or discussion.

(5) It is equally advantageous to the teacher to determine the foremost obstacle to his achieving his chosen objective. Again, one to a customer. Is it inattention, complexity, quantity, or embarrassment? Whose embarrassment — the students' or the teacher's, or both? Boredom — the teacher's or the students', or both? What is the basic obstacle blocking the teacher from conveying his subject?

(6) What is at stake? Is what the teacher intends to teach important, urgent, necessary, crucial? Teachers teach better and students learn better when what is being taught matters. I tell my acting students that there really is only one stake — life and death. An actor plays his role most compellingly when he creates an objective so important that if he does not achieve it for the character, the character's life will not be worth living. Can you imagine how meaningful each lesson would be if the teaching of it on the part of the teacher and the learning of it on the part of the students meant the difference between having or not having the lives they want to live? I am exaggerating a bit here; but striving for the dramatic effect is an occupational hazard. Yet I am certain that there is an inextricable connection between a teacher's ability to make his topic deeply significant to his own life and the lives of his students and his success as a teacher.

(7) Finally, the actor and the teacher must choose the most effective tactics for achieving their objectives. I teach my acting students to find action words, transitive verbs with which to pursue their objectives. The secret of powerful acting is to discover and communicate what the character is doing — not what the character is saying. Characters in plays do not talk to each other; they pursue their objectives by perpetrating action. They do things to each other.

(8) Wouldn't teaching and learning any subject be more satisfying if the lessons moved the teacher and his students to act, as opposed to involving them in simply speaking and listening to facts, figures, or formulas? A teacher might do well to ask himself while he is preparing his classes, "What do I want this lesson to enable my students to do?" Then he could choose specific tactics to encourage his students to take action. He could divide

each lesson into sections intended specifically to comfort them, entertain them, surprise them, enlighten them, remind them, reinforce them, and praise them. He could also choose a summary tactic for each class that contributed to a climactic structure for the entire course, thus allowing the course to build to the teacher's desired conclusion.

(9) At the end of a course, a teacher might test his students' assimilation of the material by providing them with the opportunity to take action using what he has shared. Instead of their stating the information solely linguistically in the form of a paper or a written exam, perhaps they could also demonstrate their comprehension by achieving a chosen goal appropriate to the subject matter. Each individual teacher will be the best judge of what endeavors to encourage.

(10) When the students do this, they, too, will become actors. Their actor-teacher will have helped them become actor-students. As did their teacher, they will benefit from knowing what they want, what they must confront, why what they want is important, and how, specifically, they will go about getting it. They might keep in mind the subject of my essay, the four rudiments of acting technique: (1) the objective; (2) the obstacle; (3) the stake; and (4) the tactics.

Testimonial 17
Roger Soenksen
Department of Human Communication
James Madison University
Harrisonburg, Virginia 22801

(1) My experiences as an actor began in a production at my junior college and continued throughout my undergraduate education. I have drawn upon those experiences as a professor. Principles of acting are truly applicable in the classroom. This testimonial will demonstrate how I utilize some key concepts of acting.

(2) Preparation was consistently emphasized by the various directors that I had the pleasure to work with during my acting career. Time would be invested repeating stage blocking and practicing lines. In teaching I have also found that "preparation prevents poor performance." Time is well spent planning lectures, anticipating when visual aids would be helpful, and practicing the best way to organize the lecture material.

(3) A second important acting skill is enthusiasm. One of my undergraduate faculty directors indicated that even if we deliver the same lines over and over, our voices need to communicate a high level of interest because members of our audience may only see one performance. The director emphasized that you never want to send an audience home

disappointed because of a lackluster performance. Teaching also requires vocal inflection and a high level of enthusiasm. I rewrite all my lectures each year. This helps me to keep my enthusiasm high, and students can see from my nonverbal activities that I'm excited teaching my subject matter. I try never to have students leave a lecture feeling that "I wish the professor would be more lively and interesting."

(4) A third aspect of acting that has proven valuable in teaching is researching my subject. As stated earlier, I never deliver the same lecture twice. During acting class, my professors stressed the need to "package the scene." They meant that each scene had to include all the key elements performed in concert. Students in my class demand the same kind of packaging. I continually ask myself, Where did the lecture drag? Are the statistics the most recent available? Are the visual aids helpful? Can the students relate to the illustrations I utilize? I have found that making quick notes at the conclusion of each class is helpful in recalling trouble spots in my lecture.

(5) I have found that my nonverbal delivery is an important teaching tool and a fourth important aspect in effective teaching. I teach classes ranging from one hundred to twenty students. This requires that I vary my vocal inflections according to the size of the room that I'm lecturing in as well as the number of students that I am addressing. Students who can't easily hear you will daydream. Also, the voice should create the appropriate atmosphere in the classroom. I can express a wide variety of emotions with the use of my voice which I have found to be effective in communicating my feelings on a particular topic.

(6) The final aspect of teaching that I have found helpful is the presentation of my lecture material in an argumentative form much like a playwright employs. The fourfold process I utilize includes:

1. Label the material
2. Explain the material
3. Support the material
4. Conclude the material.

I have found that it helps to have my lecture material begin with a short statement that allows my students to take more accurate notes. I then offer my explanation of the meaning of this short label in language that the students can easily comprehend. I am then able to develop specific instances, illustrations, examples, statistics, and so forth, to help support the argument that I am advancing as my main idea. The final aspect of any lecture is to repeat the key concept to reemphasize the importance of the information through repetition.

(7) The use of these acting principles has worked for me in teaching

college students. However, there is no sure formula or quick and easy way to become a good teacher. The key to success is hard work and a love of the profession.

Testimonial 18
Trudy Steuernagel
Coordinator of Women's Studies
Political Science Department
Kent State University
Kent, Ohio 44242

(1) I never thought of myself as an actor or the classroom as a stage, but clearly there are techniques I use that are shared with fellow performers. For me, the single most important thing I do in my political theory courses, aside from knowing the texts, is to position myself in respect to my students. My entire teaching career has been spent in a large state university. Most of the classrooms are, at best, impersonal. What I strive to do is create a sense of intimacy in the classroom. I want the students to care about each other and to care about the material. I want them to think there is a sense of urgency about what they are studying and that these classical texts in political theory can, if they open themselves to them, affect the future direction of their lives.

(2) It is not unusual for me to have fifty students in an introduction to political theory class. Since I emphasize class discussion, the creation of a sense of intimacy is particularly important, especially to those students who are uncomfortable speaking in front of a large number of people. I have found the following techniques useful. I am the only audio-visual aid. I remain firmly committed to a minimalist approach to teaching, and despite my recognition that many of this generation of students expect some kind of electronic enhancement, I make no concessions, no excuses (although it is true I am unable to operate a film projector, overhead projector, video or audio cassette recorder. I am somewhat more skilled at unrolling maps, and occasionally I will attempt to indicate the location of Thrace), and no apologies.

(3) I use a podium resting on a table to hold some notes. I try to refer to them as infrequently as possible. This frees me to roam the room. I always do this during the lecture part of the class. I will often, if the room is long and shallow, position myself at one corner or the other for some extended periods of time. This directs student attention to me. I also try to match my pacing speed to my vocal speed. If, for example, I am setting the stage for a discussion of Plato's allegory of the cave, I will speak in hushed tones and pace very deliberately, attempting to create a mood for the students to place

themselves in the cave, to imagine the flickering firelight and the macabre puppet show. As our discussion moves to the movement from the cave to the sunlight, I will all but run across the room, arms uplifted, and voice soaring. This works *only* if you are confident of your knowledge of the text. If you have to sneak a peek at your notes, the spell is broken.

(4) When I am interested in greater student involvement during the discussion part of the class, I try to make myself as unobtrusive as possible. This is not too difficult since I am anything but a compelling physical presence. I will often sit on the table, pull my legs under me, and lean forward. At this stage I want to listen and be a part of the group. I try not to do anything that would distract attention from the student who is speaking.

(5) I use variations of these techniques in all of my classes and, for the most part, have been rewarded with an exciting classroom atmosphere. A word of caution, however. I have also fallen over wastebaskets, knocked a map stand into a window, and bumped my shins on any number of inanimate offenders. The use of classroom space to enhance teaching has its dark side.

REFERENCES

Abrami, P. C., Leventhal, L., and Perry, R. P. 1982. Educational seduction. *Review of Educational Research* 52: 446–64.

Andersen, J. F. 1986. Instructor nonverbal communication: Listening to our silent messages. *New Directions for Teaching and Learning* 26: 41–49.

Andersen, J., and Withrow, J. 1987. The impact of lecturer nonverbal expressiveness on improving mediated instruction. *Communication Education* 30 (4): 242–53.

Anderson, V. 1977. *Training the speaking voice.* New York: Oxford University Press.

Armour, R. 1975. Humor in the classroom. *Independent School District* 35 (1): 61.

Arnold, G. B. 1990. The teacher and nonverbal communication. *The Political Science Teacher* 3 (3): 3–5.

Bandura, A. 1986. *Social foundations of thought and action.* Englewood Cliffs, N.J.: Prentice Hall.

Barcinas, S. J., and Gozer, M. D. 1986. Dramatization as a teaching technique in work orientation. *Passages* 2 (1): 54–57.

Barto, D. 1986. *Teacher as actor — Henry David Thoreau: From room one-eleven to Walden Pond and beyond.* Paper presented at the meeting of the National Council of Teachers of English, Philadelphia.

Baughman, M. D. 1979. Teaching with humor: A performing art. *Contemporary Education* 51 (1): 26–30.

Bettencourt, E., Gillett, M., and Hull, J. 1983. Effects of teacher enthusiasm training on student on-task behavior and achievement. *American Educational Research Journal* 20 (3): 435–50.

Billson, J. M., and Tiberius, R. G. 1991. Effectual social arrangements for teaching and learning. In R. J. Menges and M. D. Svinicki, eds., *College teaching: From theory to practice,* pp. 87–109. San Francisco: Jossey-Bass.

Bradley, B. E. 1981. *Fundamentals of speech communication.* Dubuque, Iowa: Wm. C. Brown.

Brigham, F. J. 1991. *Generating excitement: Teacher enthusiasm and students with learning difficulties.* Paper presented at the Annual Meeting of the Council for Learning Disabilities, Minneapolis.

Brophy, J., and Good, T. 1986. Teacher behavior and student achievement. In M. Wittrock, ed., *Handbook of research on teaching*, pp. 328–75). New York: Macmillan.

Browne, M. N., and Keeley, S. M. 1985. Achieving excellence: Advice to new teachers. *College Teaching* 33 (2): 78–83.

Bruner, J. S. 1960. *The process of education*. Cambridge: Harvard University Press.

Bryant, J., Comisky, P., Crane, J., and Zillmann, D. 1980. Relationship between college teachers' use of humour in the classroom and students' evaluations of their teachers. *Journal of Educational Psychology* 72 (4): 511–19.

Bryant, J., Comisky, P., and Zillmann, D. 1979. Teachers' humor in the college classroom. *Communication Education* 23 (28): 110–18.

Bryant, J., and Zillmann, D. 1988. Using humor to promote learning in the classroom. *Journal of Children in Contemporary Society* 20 (1–2): 49–78.

Burts, C. C., et al. 1985. Effects of teacher enthusiasm on three- and four-year-old children's acquisition of four concepts. *Theory and Research in Social Education* 13 (1): 19–29.

Butler, L., Miezitis, S., Friedman, R., and Cole, E. 1980. The effect of two school-based intervention programs on depressive symptoms in preadolescents. *American Educational Research Journal* 17 (1): 111–19.

Campbell, C. P. 1981. Characteristics of effective vocational instructors. *Canadian Vocational Journal* 16 (4): 24–28.

Carroll, J. 1991. Teacher's personality swings from likable to arrogant, testy. *Erie Times-News*, March 24, p. N-1.

Chirpich, T. P. 1977. Ideal and non-ideal gases: An experiment with surprise value. *Journal of Chemical Education* 54 (1): 378–79.

Civikly, J. M. 1986. *Communicating in college classrooms. New Directions for Teaching and Learning*, no. 26. San Francisco: Jossey-Bass.

Collins, M. L. 1981. *PHI DELTA KAPPAN Newsletter* (June).

Comisky, P., and Bryant, J. 1982. Factors involved in generating suspense. *Human Communication Research* 9 (1): 49–58.

Conquergood, D. 1993. Storied worlds and the work of teaching. *Communication Education* 42 (4): 337–48.

Cornett, C. E. 1986. *Learning through laughter: Humor in the classroom. Fastback 241.* Bloomington, Ind.: Phi Delta Kappan Foundation.

Dead Poets' Society. 1989. Touchstone Pictures.

Dembo, M. H. 1988. *Applying educational psychology in the classroom*. New York: Longman.

Demetrulias, D. A. M. 1982. Gags, giggles, guffaws: Using cartoons in the classroom. *Journal of Reading* 26 (1): 66–68.

Dinkmeyer, D., McKay, G. D., and Dinkmeyer, D., Jr. 1980. *Systematic training for effective teaching (STET)*. Circle Pines, Minn.: American Guidance Services, Inc.

Dolle, D., and Willems G. M. 1984. The communicative approach to foreign language teaching. In G. M. Willems, ed., *Communicative foreign language teaching and the training of foreign language teachers*, pp. 85–102. Bloomington, Ind.: Viewpoints.

Donald, J. G., and Sullivan, A. M. 1985. *Using research to improve teaching*. San Francisco: Jossey-Bass.

Duncombe, S., and Heikkinen, M. 1988. Role-playing for different viewpoints. *English Journal* 36 (1): 3–5.

Eison, J. 1990. Confidence in the classroom. *College Teaching* 38 (1): 21–25.

Enerson, D. M., and Plank, K. M. 1993. *The Penn State teacher*. University Park: Pennsylvania State University,

Festinger, L. A. 1957. *A theory of cognitive dissonance*. Evanston, Ill.: Row, Peterson.

Fisch, L. 1991. Further confessions of a closet thespian. *Connexions* (Fall), p. 1.

French, J., Jr., and Raven, B. 1960. The bases for social power. In D. Cartwright, and J. Zander, eds., *Group dynamics: Research and theory*. Evanston, Ill.: Row, Peterson.

Frymier, A. B., and Thompson, C. A. 1992. Perceived teacher affinity-seeking in relation to perceived teacher credibility. *Communication Education* 41 (4): 388–99.

Geske, J. 1992. Overcoming the drawbacks of the large lecture class. *College Teaching* 40 (4): 151–54.

Gillett, M. 1980. *The effects of teacher enthusiasm on the at-task behavior of students in elementary grades*. ERIC Accession Number ED 202 823.

Glover, J. A., and Bruning, R. H. 1990. *Educational psychology*. Boston: Little, Brown and Company.

Goor, M. 1989. *Humor in the classroom: Options for enhancing learning*. Paper presented at the National Conference of the Council for Exceptional Children/Council for Children with Behavior Disorders, September, Charlotte, N.C.

Gorham, J., and Christophel, D. M. 1990. The relationship of teachers' use of humor in the classroom to immediacy and student learning. *Communication Education* 39 (1): 46–62.

Goulden, N. R. 1991. *Improving instructors' speaking skills*. Idea Paper no. 24, Center for Faculty Evaluation and Development, Kansas State University, Manhattan.

Grant, B. M., and Hennings, D. G. 1971. *The teacher moves: An analysis of nonverbal activity*. New York: Teachers College Press.

Grobe, R. P., Pettibone, T. J., and Martin, D. W. 1973. Effects of lecturer pace on noise level in a university classroom. *The Journal of Educational Research* 67 (2): 73–75.

Guilford, P. 1959. The structure of the intellect. *Psychological Bulletin* 53 (4): 267–93.

Hall, E. T. 1966. *The hidden dimension*. New York: Doubleday.

Hanning, R. W. 1984. The classroom as theater of self: Some observations for beginning teachers. *ADE Bulletin* 77: 33–37.

Herbert, P. J. 1991. *Humor in the classroom: Theories, functions, and guidelines*. Paper presented at the Annual Meeting of the Central States Communication Association, April, Chicago.

Hesler, M. W. 1972. An investigation of instructor use of space. *Dissertation Abstracts International* 33: 3055A (University Microfilms no. 72-30,905).

Highet, G. 1950. *The art of teaching*. New York: Random House (Vintage).

Holloway, G., Abbot-Chapman, J., and Hughes, P. 1992. *Identifying the qualities and characteristics of the effective teacher, Report 2, Normative dimensions of teacher/student interaction*. Youth Education Studies Centre, University of Tasmania, Hobart, Tasmania.

Hook, S. 1981. Morris R. Cohen—Fifty years later. In J. Epstein, Jr., ed., *Masters: Portraits of great teachers*. New York: Basic Books.

House, P. A. 1988. Components of success in mathematics and science. *School Science and Mathematics* 88 (8): 632–41.

Humphreys, B. R. 1990. *A cheerful heart is good medicine: The emotional and physical benefits of humor.* Doctoral research paper. Biola University, California. ERIC Accession Number ED 317-892.

Hunsaker, J. S. 1988. It's no joke: Using humor in the classroom. *The Clearing House* 61 (6): 285.

Hurt, H. R., Scott, M. D., and McCroskey, J. C. 1978. *Communication in the classroom.* Reading, Mass.: Knopf.

Javidi, M., Downs, V. C., and Nussbaum, J. F. 1988. A comparative analysis of teachers' use of dramatic style behaviors at higher and secondary education levels. *Communication Education* 37 (4): 278–88.

Johnson, B. D. 1991. Great Teachers. *Maclean's* 104 (42): 34–35.

Johnson, D. R. 1973. The element of surprise: An effective classroom technique. *Mathematics Teacher* 66 (1): 13–16.

Jones, F. H. 1987. *Positive classroom discipline.* New York: McGraw-Hill.

Jordan, J. R. 1982. The professor as communicator. *Improving College and University Teaching* 30 (3): 120–24.

Jose, P. E., and Brewer, W. F. 1990. Early grade school children's liking of script and suspense story structures. *Journal of Reading Behavior* 22 (4): 355–72.

Justen, E. F. 1984. The missing link in ESL teacher training. *MEXTESOL Journal* 8 (2): 49–62.

Keiper, R. W. 1991. *The teacher as actor.* Paper presented at the 71st Annual Meeting of the Association of Teacher Educators, New Orleans.

Kelly, N., and Kelly, B. 1982. *Backgrounds, education, and teaching styles of award-winning professors.* Annual Meeting of the Rocky Mountain Educational Research Association, Albuquerque, N.M. ERIC Accession Number ED 230 080.

Kelser, J. E. 1988. The role of surprise in the organic laboratory. *Journal of Chemical Education* 65 (1): 78–79.

Klein, J., and Fitch, M. 1990. First grade children's comprehension of "noodle doodle box." *Youth Theatre Journal* 5 (2): 7–13.

Knapp, M. L 1971. The role of non-verbal communication in the classroom. *Theory into Practice* 10 (4): 243–49.

Korobkin, D. 1988. Humor in the classroom: Considerations and strategies. *College Teaching* 36 (4): 154–58.

Kounin, J. 1970. *Discipline and group management.* New York: Holt, Rinehart, & Winston.

Krathwohl, D. R., Bloom, B. S., and Masia, B. B. 1956. *Taxonomy of educational objectives. Handbook II: Affective domain.* New York: David McKay.

Kress, G. C., and Ehrlichs, M. A. 1990. Development of confidence in child behavior management through role-playing. *Journal of Dental Education* 54 (10):, 619–22.

Kurre, J. 1993. The art of teaching. Speech presented to Penn State-Behrend faculty, Erie, Penna.

Larson, G. 1982. Humorous teaching makes serious learning. *TETYC* 8 (3): 197–99.

Lowe, D. W. 1991. *Using cartoons in psychology lectures: The "far side" of psychology.* Paper presented at the Thirteenth Annual National Institute on the Teaching of Psychology Conference, Tampa.

Lowman, J. 1984. *Mastering the techniques of teaching.* San Francisco: Jossey-Bass.

MacAdam, B. 1985. Humor in the classroom: Implications for the bibliographic instruction librarian. *College & Research Libraries* 46 (4): 327–33.

MacLaren, R., and Olson, D. 1993. Trick or treat: Children's understanding of surprise. *Cognitive Development* 8 (1): 27–46.

Magnan, B. 1989. 147 practical tips for teaching professors. Madison, Wisc.: Magna Publications.

Manghue, R. E. 1980. Props for the beginning accounting classroom. *Business Education Forum* 35 (3): 14–16.

Mark, J. L. 1989. Twenty-two good educational practices. *Adult Literacy and Basic Education* 13 (1): 45–51.

McKeachie, W. J. 1986. *Teaching tips: A guidebook for the beginning college teacher.* Lexington, Mass.: D. C. Heath.

Meier, R. S., and Feldhusen, J. F. 1979. Another look at Dr. Fox: Effect of stated purpose on evaluation, lecturer expressiveness, and density of lecture content on student ratings. *Journal of Educational Psychology* 71 (3): 339–45.

Meyer, W. U., Niepel, M., Rudolph, U., and Schutzwohl, A. 1991. An experimental analysis of surprise. *Cognition and Emotion* 5 (4): 295–311.

Murray, D. M. 1984. Writing and teaching for surprise. *College English* 46 (1): 1–7.

Murray, H. G. 1985. Classroom teaching behaviors related to college teaching effectiveness. In J. G. Donald and A. M. Sullivan, eds., *Using research to improve teaching,* pp. 21–34. San Francisco: Jossey-Bass.

Neilsen, D. L. F. 1993. *Humor scholarship: A research bibliography.* Westport, Conn.: Greenwood Press.

Neuliep, J. W. 1991. An examination of the content of high school teachers' humor in the classroom and the development of an inductively derived taxonomy of classroom humor. *Communication Education* 40 (4): 343–55.

"Not so rich, or famous." 1993. *NEA Today* 12 (4): 25.

Nussbaum, J. F. 1992. Effective teacher behaviors. *Communication Education* 41 (2): 167–80.

Nussbaum, J. F., Comadena, M. E., and Holladay, S. J. 1987. Classroom verbal behavior of highly effective teachers. *Journal of Thought* 22: 73–80.

Ostrand, J., and Creaser, J. 1978. Development of counselor candidate dominance in three learning conditions. *The Journal of Psychology* 99: 199–202.

"Our readers write." 1982. *English Journal* 71 (2): 68–76.

Palmer, P. J. 1990. Good teaching: A matter of living the mystery. *Change* 22 (1): 11–15.

Penner, J. G. 1984. *Why many college teachers cannot lecture.* Springfield, Ill.: Charles C. Thomas.

Perry, R. P. 1985. Instructor expressiveness: Implications for improving teaching. In J. G. Donald and A. M. Sullivan, eds., *Using research to improve teaching* (35–49). San Francisco: Jossey-Bass.

Peterson, I. 1980. Humor in the physics classroom. *The Physics Teacher* 18 (9): 646–49.

Phi Delta Kappan. 1991. 72 (7): 501.

Powell, J. P., and Anderson, L. W. 1985. Humour and teaching in higher education. *Studies in Higher Education* 10 (1): 79–90.

Puckett, M. J., and Shaw, J. M. 1988. The storytime exchange: Ways to enhance it. *Childhood Education* 64 (5): 293–98.

Ramsell, B. 1978. The poetic experience of surprise and the art of teaching. *The English Journal* 67 (5): 22–25.

Richmond, V. P., Gorham, J. S., and McCroskey, J. C. 1987. The relationship between selected immediacy behaviors and cognitive learning. In M. McLaughlin, ed., *Communication yearbook 10*, pp. 574–90. Beverly Hills: Sage.

Robinson, W. K. 1993. Dramatic arts for teachers: Preparing prospective teachers to take center stage. Paper presented at the National Association of Teacher Educators meeting, Los Angeles.

Rosenshine, B., and Furst, R. 1973. The use of direct observation to study teaching. In R. Travers, ed., *Second handbook on research on teaching*. Chicago: Rand McNally.

Rubin, L. J. 1985. *Artistry in teaching*. New York: Random House.

Sallinen-Kuparinen, A., Marttinen, P., Permamaki, P., and Porhola, M. 1987. In A. Sallinen-Kuparinen, ed., *Perspectives on instructional communication*, pp. 97–111. Publication of the Department of Communication 5, Jyvaskyla, Finland: University of Jyvaskyla.

Schwartz, L. L. 1980. Criteria for effective university teaching. *Improving College and University Teaching* 28 (3): 120–23.

Shedlock, M. L. 1951. *The art of the story-teller*. New York: Dover.

Smith, H. A. 1979. Nonverbal communication in teaching. *Review of Educational Research* 49 (4): 631–72.

Soenksen, R. 1992. *Confessions of a professor, nee actor*. Paper presented at the Speech Communication National Convention, Chicago.

Sommer, R. 1969. *Personal space: The behavioral basis of design*. Englewood Cliffs, N.J.: Prentice-Hall.

Sprague, J. 1993. Why teaching works: The transformative power of pedagogical communication. *Communication Education* 42 (4): 349–66.

Starratt, R. J. 1990. *The drama of schooling/The schooling of drama*. New York: The Falmer Press.

Streeter, B. B. 1986. The effects of training experienced teachers in enthusiasm on students' attitudes toward reading. *Reading Psychology* 7 (4): 249–59.

Strine, M. S. 1993. Of boundaries, borders, and contact zones: Author(iz)ing pedagogical practices. *Communication Education* 42 (4): 367–76.

Sukow, W. W. 1990. Physical science workshops for teachers using interactive science exhibits. *School Science and Mathematics* 90 (1): 42–47.

Sullivan, R. L. 1992. It's a H.I.T. *Vocational Education Journal* 67 (3): 36–38.

Tamborini, R., and Zillmann, D. 1981. College students' perceptions of lectures using humor. *Perceptual and Motor Skills* 52 (2): 417–32.

Tauber, R. T. 1990. *Classroom management from A to Z*. Fort Worth: Harcourt Brace College Publishers.

Timpson, W. M. 1982. *Teaching as performing*. Englewood Cliffs, N.J.: Prentice-Hall.

Tobin, K. 1986. Effects of teacher wait-time on discourse characteristics in mathematics and language arts classes. *American Educational Research Journal* 23 (2): 191–200.

Travers, R. M. 1979. Training the teacher as a performing artist. *Contemporary Education* 51 (1): 14–18.

Travers, R. M., and Dillon, J. 1975. *The making of a teacher: A plan for professional self-development*. New York: Macmillan.

Vidler, D. C., and Levine, J. 1981. Curiosity, magic, and the teacher. *Education* 101 (3): 273–75.

Vizmuller, J. 1980. Psychological reasons for using humor in a pedagogical setting. *Canadian Modern Language Review* 36 (2): 266–71.

Walter, G. 1990. Laugh teacher laugh. *Teaching for Excellence* 9 (8): 28–29.

Walz, J. C. 1986. Increasing student talk time in the foreign language classroom. *Canadian Modern Language Review* 42 (5): 952–67.

Wandersee, J. H. 1982. Humor as a teaching strategy. *American Biology Teacher* 44 (4): 212–18.

Warnock, P. 1989. Humor as a didactic tool in adult education. *Lifelong Learning* 12 (8): 22–24.

Weaver, R. L. 1981. Effective lecturing techniques. *The Clearing House* 55: 20–23.

Weimer, M. 1993. *Improving your classroom teaching*, Survival Skills for Scholars Series. Newbury Park, Calif: SAGE.

Wells, E. F. 1979. Bewitched, dazzled, and delighted. *Teacher* 96 (9): 53–54.

Welsz, E. 1990. Energizing the classroom. *College Teaching* 38 (2): 74–76.

Witty, P. 1950. Some characteristics of the effective teacher. *Educational Administration and Supervision* 36: 193–208.

Wlodkowski, R. J. 1985. *Enhancing adult motivation to learn*. San Francisco: Jossey-Bass.

Woods, P. 1983. Coping at school through humour. *British Journal of Education* 4 (2): 111–24.

Woolfolk, A. E. 1993. *Educational psychology*, 5th ed. Englewood Cliffs, N.J.: Prentice-Hall.

Wulff, D. H. 1993. Tales of transformation: Applying a teaching effectiveness perspective to stories about teaching. *Communication Education* 42 (4): 377–97.

Zillmann, D., and Hay, T. A. 1975. The effect of suspense and its resolutions on the appreciation of dramatic presentations. *Journal of Research in Personality* 9 (4): 307–23.

Ziv, A. 1989. Using humor to develop creative thinking. *Journal of Children in Contemporary Society* 20 (1–2): 99–116.

INDEX

About the Authors

ROBERT T. TAUBER is Professor of Education at The Behrend College of Penn State at Erie. He has written and published extensively on classroom management and oral communication skills for both students and teachers.

CATHY SARGENT MESTER is Instructor in Speech Communication at The Behrend College of Penn State at Erie. Her research in the areas of communication education and religious communication has resulted in the publication of two books, several scholarly articles, and over thirty conference and convention papers.

ISBN 0-275-94823-4

90000>

EAN

9 780275 948238

HARDCOVER BAR CODE